SOLD OUT!

How I survived a year of not shopping

Robert Llewellyn

GAIA
THINKING

An Hachette Livre UK Company
www.hachettelivre.co.uk

First published in Great Britain in 2008 by
Gaia, a division of Octopus Publishing Group Ltd
2-4 Heron Quays, London E14 4JP
www.octopusbooks.co.uk

ISBN 978-1-85675-308-1

A CIP catalogue record for this book is available from the British Library

Printed and bound in Italy

Printed on Cyclus Offset, a 100 per cent recycled paper

10 9 8 7 6 5 4 3 2 1

Executive Editor: Sandra Rigby
Managing Editor: Clare Churly
Executive Art Editor: Mark Stevens
Page make-up: Dorchester Typesetting Group Ltd
Senior Production Controller: Simone Nauerth

'An unexamined life is a life not worth living'
Socrates

'Been examining mine in such minute detail
I suppose it must have been worth living
for at least one year'
Robert Llewellyn

Foreword

MY FIRST problem with Robert not buying anything for a year was I thought he didn't buy that much to begin with. He already looked like a tramp before the year started. In the November before, when our daughter and I saw him on telly with a hole in the armpit of his ancient black cardigan (£25, Top Man, 1995), I thought, 'This is ridiculous,' and said supportive-wife things like, 'Why don't you give up something really difficult, or do something challenging, like not getting angry with the kids on a Saturday morning or not laughing at my misfortunes so gleefully?'

I could understand seeing how much money you could spend in a year, or spending a year buying things you didn't need, then writing a book about it, but I didn't get not buying stuff for a year and writing about that. I mean, what would you say – 'Didn't buy new undies today and felt virtuous'? (You can see how much support Robert got at home from loved ones.) Anyway, I thought we'd done all that not buying stuff for more than a year in our youth – I certainly had, or more like three decades, out of necessity. I know that feeling very well, as does Robert.

I could also understand the bit about being more ecologically sensitive. But then you should do that all the time, with the occasional exception when you need to be frivolous. There's nothing wrong with a bit of frivolity; it's certainly better than not buying things because you feel guilty about spending the money. As a good Catholic girl, I've had to learn how to buy something that isn't necessarily on special offer and then assure everyone of its cheapness the minute it is admired.

I suppose I was interested to know if we'd be better off at the end of the year. Probably not, I thought, because blokes aren't that interested in shopping. But there again, I would never buy a new car or top-of-the-range digital camera or three Apple Macs in a year, which is just the sort of thing a bloke does. The truth is, when he spends, a 50-year-old man spends a lot. You can't rack up that many bills on scented candles and cushions, especially if you wait for the Parlane sale and get everything for two quid (once a Catholic), whereas a new car ...

There is a New Age theory that money is energy and it has to flow, while the capitalists say you have to speculate to accumulate. Well, most of us are too frightened to find out if that's true, but I think they've got a point. It doesn't justify wanton consumerism and all the complications of owning too much stuff, or deny the fact that the planet has finite resources so we shouldn't consume recklessly. But where does that leave you? You are going to spend money on stuff that makes a difference to your life and to the lives of others around you. What else? Your garden ... art ... food ... goods and services from local people ...

What I didn't like was the part that felt like it was about deprivation. Robert's not an extravagant person anyway and if you deprive yourself it's harder to give – well, it is for me. As the year went on, he became more and more tyrannical and petty – the not spending certainly didn't make him a joyous person. In the end, I thought, 'Why didn't you just do the normal mid-life crisis thing and buy a sports car?' And then I got it. 'Llewellyn,' I said, 'this looks to me suspiciously like an excuse to draw attention to yourself – again.'

Judy Pascoe

Introduction

BEFORE I go any further with this I have to make an important statement: nothing in this book is made up. I'm not writing a story; I am explaining a part of my life which, almost despite my best efforts, has changed the way I now look at the world.

In the true style of the evangelist, I am nervously shuffling towards the notion that if I can explain this internal and personal change, it might encourage one or two other people to consider similar aspects of their own life. Which, to be honest, is often the underlying – and regularly denied – aim of many of the cheap, shallow show-offs you see on telly or in stand-up comedy venues.

However, because of the nature of my past work, I can see that there might be some doubt as to the veracity of what I say. I have stood on hundreds of stages in front of thousands of people and told thousands of stories that are not always 100 per cent true. They might have been based on an event or incorporate a certain amount of truth, but they will have been embroidered in the sometimes desperate pursuit of a big noisy laugh from the audience. I have also written books that contain entirely made-up stories, none of which were even based on anything that actually happened to me or anyone I know.

Despite that, though, something happened a few years ago that prompted me to try and clarify things now. In 1996 I wrote a very different sort of book called *Thin He Was and Filthy-haired*, which was entirely true. In it I recalled events that had happened to me 20-odd years previously, when I was a fledgling hippie in the squats and colleges of Oxford. Although this book garnered more flattering reviews in highbrow newspapers than anything I have ever written, it sold very slowly. That is, it didn't sell very many copies. Other books I have written which were totally ignored by the literati sold by the ship-load, but that's not what this is about.

One reviewer, Giles Coren, whom I have always thought of as a food critic, wrote a lovely review of *Thin He Was and Filthy-haired* in the *Sunday Times*. I'll quote a bit, not to show off, just to illustrate the point. Well, OK, to show off a bit, but when you've read it, you'll realize it's not showing off that much:

> The fact that Robert Llewellyn is a comedian does blur one minor issue: one is never quite sure if the Robert of the book is Robert Llewellyn ... Are we to suspend our disbelief here or not? If it is absolutely God's honest truth, then it is hilarious ... If it is entirely fabricated, then how strange, for it is by no means side-splitting stuff.

Good call, Giles. So, I am taking note and wish to point out that although I am by definition a show-off, a shallow showman, a story-teller, a fabricator of mistruth and an embroiderer of minuscule moments, this book is about what really took place during one year in my life. If anything, I am holding back more information than I am giving, because this was a very difficult year for me which had little to do with not buying anything, save that I didn't even have the escape of feeling momentarily good about myself because I was wearing new socks. It was a year of not getting out of anything, a year of having nowhere to turn, not even a cheap joke to avoid the difficulties I was faced with.

So, Giles, if you ever read this, not that I imagine you will – perhaps I should add some rubbish recipes at the end – it is a true book. The Robert in this book is me.

**'Day 1: Woke up, didn't buy anything,
felt a bit miffed.'**

BEFORE any tales of how hard it was to live for a year without new socks, the most important thing to state right now is I am not some eco-aware, caring, charity-working, humanitarian man with a mission to save the world. I am a selfish, lazy, greedy consumer who has compromised his once firmly held beliefs beyond the point of redemption.

Just wanted to clear that up.

Now that my year of not shopping, or, as I referred to it, 'making do', is over, I find it hard to believe that I actually did refrain from buying anything new for myself for a full calendar year. However, I really did do it, even though when I started the whole silly project I had no idea that a simple decision made on the spur of the moment, without any forethought, would raise so many complicated issues.

If I'm honest, my decision was made during a bit of an immature sulk. The initial notion was very simple and I'll go into why I did it later, but all I decided to do was to completely stop shopping for anything other than food and medicine. Not forever – I was old enough to know that would just be silly. I simply decided not to buy anything new for myself for one calendar year.

To try and explain, the fact that I was wearing worn-out socks, undies that had seen better days, trousers with patches and shoes with holes in was in many ways the least of my problems. I admit that not buying an iPhone when it came out during the year, not upgrading my computer and not trading in my worn-out car for a new one all became a bit of a drudge as the year went on. Having to get things repaired instead of throwing them away and buying new ones became an expensive ordeal, but none of it was that hard. If you think you are going to read about someone who really suffered deprivation from not shopping for a year, prepare to be let down. It was what happened internally that was difficult, it was having nowhere to turn that was painful.

I made this decision after a mundane and painless shopping spree in a giant shopping mall, I mean a really huge one. I may as well spell it out right at the start: shopping malls bring me no pleasure; they don't even bring a vague feeling of happiness. I can't remain neutral about shopping malls. I just hate them. I was in the mall with my family, my Australian wife, Judy, and my two children, Holly, 11, and Louis, 14.

Obviously they loved being in a shopping mall buying things. I was the only grumpy one in the party.

So, the following morning, I made my decision while on a solitary walk. I would just stop buying stuff. Nothing for a whole year.

The initial result of this decision was startling: I felt immediate and palpable relief. I wouldn't have to wonder if I should or shouldn't buy anything, if I could or couldn't afford it, if I should wait until that cheque finally arrived from the BBC or borrow the money now. All those thoughts could be utterly banished for a year and I could think about something else.

Brilliant.

This euphoria was quickly followed by deep anxiety. As I mulled it over, I wondered how hard it would be to truly not buy anything new for a whole year. Although by the time you reach my age you realize that your damn parents were actually right when they said time passes faster as you get older, a whole year stretching ahead of me seemed like a very long time.

Would I find that I just couldn't go for that long without buying a new pair of socks – one of my biggest fears – or that some new computer or cool gizmo would be launched that I somehow felt I couldn't live without?

I checked myself – something I tend to do during long walks. It was ridiculous. Surely there was nothing I needed that badly. I would just have to make do with what I had and not moan on about it.

I started formulating rules to live by, on reflection a slightly pathetic last-ditch attempt at gaining some control over my life when I felt all control had slipped away while I wasn't looking.

Not shopping for one whole year couldn't be that hard, really. In fact I decided that it wasn't much of a challenge at all. I have never been that good at shopping anyway, in the sense that buying a new thing doesn't seem to give me the pleasure that it clearly gives a lot of people.

This may be due to my heritage, the long thread of Protestant puritanism that I inherited through my family, although they were, to my knowledge, not very puritanical in the Oliver Cromwell sense and not in the least Protestant in the Northern Irish mode.

Most of my grandparents followed some variety of Welsh Baptist – or was it English Methodist? – thing that I have never fully understood. I truly don't know how religious they really were. I don't remember them going to church much; I can clearly remember being sent to Sunday school in the village when my grandparents were staying and they weren't at the church, which was next door. I have met deeply religious people in adult life, some wonderful and inspiring, some truly demented, but none of them really reminded me of my own grandparents.

Nonetheless, all religion aside, although I have lived most of my life furiously kicking against the things I thought my forebears stood for and believed in, I can see now that I was strongly influenced by both my parents and my grandparents.

My mother and father were of the wartime generation; my dad was 18 at the outbreak of the Second World War, a pretty suitable age to get involved in the whole damn shooting match. That's what he called the greatest international conflict the world has ever seen, a damn shooting match.

My mother was 15 at the outbreak of war and, although still a schoolgirl, she was hugely affected by rationing, bombing, the blackout, American GIs billeted across the road from her home in Cheltenham and the sacrifices she regularly told us people made without hesitation.

But rationing was the big one. My mum never really got over rationing; in fact I think she rather enjoyed it. By the time my brother, sister and I were children, in the early 1960s, rationing was a thing of the fairly recent past, but it really had finished. However, the tradition remained firmly entrenched in our family home. 'Waste not, want not', 'Make do and mend', 'Never a lender nor borrower be.'

Phrases like that were in daily use, together with 'Money doesn't grow on trees', 'A fool and his money are soon parted' and 'Money burns a hole in your pocket, my lad.' That last one was used when I had just spent two and sixpence on a box of Airfix Second World War soldiers. For those lucky enough to have been born after decimalization, two and sixpence is around twelve and a half pence, or for me at the time three weeks' pocket money.

The 'Never a lender nor borrower be' phrase caused particular confusion to my young brain, as my father worked for a building society whose sole purpose was to lend and encourage others to borrow.

We lived a frugal but not poverty-stricken existence all my childhood and I now consider myself very lucky to come from what was basically a stable home. Of course that statement ignores huge issues that our family had, hideous secrets that will never be revealed, weird behaviour that has remained unexplained, strange poverty which belied my father's income. Yes, my mum and dad had a dark secret somewhere and we, their children, truly do not know what it was; all the protagonists have taken this secret to their grave.

However, in the grand scheme of things we had a comfortable childhood, we were a fairly affectionate family and there was generally a lot of laughter in our home.

Both my parents had an enormous respect for the natural world around them. My mother had a very romantic view of rural life and nature, particularly the hills of the Cotswolds around Cheltenham, where she grew up.

Strangely, this is where I now live, and you might think it was my true desire to live my mother's dream, but in fact my wife found the house we live in and I had very little to do with it. I'm sure there is a subconscious connection there somewhere, and I do appreciate hearing the dawn chorus when I take the dog out for her morning walk, but culturally I am a total urbanite, there's no point denying it.

My parents were, more by well-entrenched habit than informed choice, very careful about the resources they had and used. They detested waste, which obviously included the overcooked green vegetables we were served on our dinner plates. You absolutely had to eat them. Now I grow my own vegetables, I am further mystified by how my mother could take such wonderful fresh produce and boil the hell out of it until it only just held its original form. Anyway, I grew up on overcooked vegetables and the cheaper cuts of meat, never drank milk and butter was spread so thin on bread you could swear there was nothing there. Waste not, want not. It was like a mantra.

I was aware even as a child that they in turn were clearly influenced by their own parents, who were of the First World War generation.

Although I have no memory of them saying such things, I know the phrases 'Know your place', 'Don't step out of line', 'Don't get too big for your boots', 'Keep your head down' and 'Be grateful for what you have' would have been common parlance for all my grandparents. If for no other reason than 70 per cent of the young men they would have known in their youth were blown to bits in the mud of northern France.

My paternal grandmother came from the Forest of Dean and was strong, strict and very clean and tidy. I don't remember being scared of her; in fact I fondly remember her and her lovely old cottage, just outside Newent in Gloucestershire. My grandfather, who lost an eye in the First World War, was a small, quiet man who loved horses.

When I think of them now, judging by present-day standards, they consumed so very little in their lives it is truly hard to imagine. I would put money on their dustbin being tiny, if they even had one. I know the path through their wonderful vegetable garden was made of cinders from the fire. I doubt they ever went to a supermarket and they left barely a stain on the planet. It is, of course, utterly unfair on ourselves to compare the way we live now with the way they did then. There was no such thing as supermarket packaging, so they didn't have to throw it away. They were also very poor and barely travelled beyond the parish. They never owned a car and certainly never went overseas unless there was a war to fight.

My parents were likewise frugal beyond belief by today's standards, but they did have cars and they shopped in supermarkets. As I have mentioned, my father worked for a building society and my mother did tireless charity work. Their dustbin was slightly bigger, but never filled. I can remember carrying it up the drive on dustbin day and it was always surprisingly light.

My mother's larder was spotless and virtually empty; the fridge always had plenty of room on the shelves, just a jug of milk and a small pack of butter. Their compost heap at the top of my father's extensive vegetable patch was very productive and they recycled everything before there was a term for it – jam jars being a good example. I know my mother never threw one away or took it to the glass-recycling bin. She filled them with jam and marmalade she made herself.

It has been an unexpected side effect of deciding to stop buying things that I have been thinking about my parents and grandparents a great deal more over the year. I suppose the connection is obvious, because I don't remember them buying anything new, ever. My parents were both dressed in second-hand clothes from charity shops, generally ones my mother worked in as an assistant. When we were children it was always 'hand-me-downs'. I can distinctly remember the first time I bought a new pair of jeans for myself when I was about 15; it was a completely novel experience. I had never before worn clothes that no one else had worn before me. This wasn't because my parents couldn't afford to buy me new clothes – the idea simply didn't occur to them. I'd wear my brother's old clothes or clothes from another slightly older child in the neighbourhood. Waste not, want not: it all makes perfect sense.

We lived in a nice enough house with a large enough garden. We had a car that came with my father's job and a

9-inch Bakelite TV set that received only the BBC, which broadcast only in black and white. We had a telephone that wasn't on a party line and we went on holidays in the summer. Once we even stayed in a hotel when touring through France – oh yes, big spenders. It was a very small, cheap hotel, but it really was a hotel and I thought it was the height of luxury.

So with all these influences, with me now at roughly the same age as my parents were then, how come I ended up with two houses, three cars, nine computers, three TVs, six phones, three bathrooms, five toilets, two washing machines, two heavy-duty dustbins, annual holidays to exclusive hotels in Italy, ski trips in the winter, constant travel to and from Australia and so many clothes that when I don't buy anything new for a year I barely notice?

Also, and here's the vital rub, if wealth and the ability to consume are a sure way to inner happiness and satisfaction, how come I am not deliriously happy in comparison with my parents and grandparents? I should be rolling on the floor in utter hysterical and perpetual joy, laughing and writhing in an ecstatic frenzy at my good fortune.

Needless to say, I am not. In fact the only surprising thing about this admission is that it isn't surprising. I think very few of us are truly under the impression that wealth equals happiness, and yet we still all strive for it.

To be fair to my generation, we grew up in a very different world from our parents. Not only that, but when I first left the parental home, I deliberately went further into poverty than they ever did. Having decided that even they were far too materialistic, I made conscious choices not to earn much money or have many possessions, and I kept it up for years.

Relatively speaking, consumer goods are fabulously cheap in comparison with 30 or 40 years ago. It is easy to be able to consume more now, and, by default, produce more waste.

The dustbin analogy is about to become painful. Grandparents: no dustbin. Parents: tiny half-empty dustbin. Us: monster double dustbins rammed so full I have to jump up and down on them to get the lids on.

Our two dustbins are enormous and so heavy that I nearly put my back out every week as I carry them up our drive for the bin operatives. Sometimes there isn't enough room inside them and I drop a couple of large black bin bags next to them.

It's important to point out that, like everyone else, we fastidiously recycle everything we can – plastic bottles, cans and jars, paper and cardboard. The difference is, we have so much stuff, we consume vast swathes every week and produce so much waste, it makes me dizzy. The really big joke about the whole thing is that we think we are the environmentally aware generation that can see the damage our forefathers have done and are trying to correct it.

Although I have always thought of myself as clued up on environmental issues, I have never stopped to look at my bins before. Taking a year out from casual consumption has made me stand on the side of the road and look at these two big black containers heavy with waste. As a family of four, we produce so much rubbish every week, most of it packaging from food.

I've been aware of it for years, but not to the extent that I am now. The simple answer is not to buy food that is surrounded by packaging; that's all we have to do. We try – during the year I have managed to reduce our waste to one very stuffed dustbin – but we don't try hard enough.

I think it's fair to say that I have been slightly obsessed with our way of life for a number of years, how it developed, it was part of my everyday thought patterns. It's very likely, therefore, that this had something to do with the initial decision. So when I got back from my walk on the day I made the decision to stop shopping, I had a shower and sat down for breakfast with Judy. I held my tongue. I have learned from 20 years together that I am an early-morning person and she is not. She has had to suffer me exploding with concepts and ideas for books, plays, films, TV shows and gardening projects at the crack of dawn and it doesn't always go down well. I tried, I really did try, not to say anything. I think I lasted about three minutes.

'Darl,' I began. (To briefly explain the word 'darl', it is the Australian short form of 'darling'. Some of my friends originally thought that Judy's name was Dhal, as in tarka dhal, the delicious Indian snack.) Anyway, 'Darl,' I said, 'I have decided that I am not going to buy anything new for a whole year.'

'That's nice, darl,' she said, and walked away without further comment.

Later in the year, Judy would have more to say about my absurd project, but clearly at that hour of the morning I could probably have said, 'Darl, I have decided it is time to cut off my penis and mail it to the Pope.' And she would have said, 'That's nice, darl.'

As in all relationships, each partner has to compromise and put up with quite a lot of nonsense from the other. In the final analysis, I think Judy has to put up with slightly more from me than I do from her.

There is one other very important statement I want to make, a warning before you read any further. This book is middle class. It's about the middle class. I do not apologize for its utterly middle-class view of the world, and although I worry that many potential readers who are not middle class will feel somewhat excluded, there is nothing I can do about it. That's what I am and the very nature of the project I undertook is by definition middle class. I go into the class debate in a later chapter, but I think it's worth bringing up here. If you are upper-class posh or working-class honourable or even low-down criminal scum, then it's doubtful you will even have read this far. If you think you're not middle class but really you are, and that accounts for about 40 per cent of middle-class people in my experience, then I urge you to read on. Of course, if you were once middle class but have adopted a low-impact, non-consuming lifestyle and you live in a small cottage on the coast of somewhere really remote, then you won't need to because you don't have to struggle with all this nonsense, and I admire you.

I have come to realize over my year of not shopping that I am far more middle class than I ever imagined. It was one of a number of realizations I didn't expect, but so much that was unexpected happened during the year.

When I decided on this little change in my life I could not have foreseen what I was in for – but I can forgive myself for that now. It is such a frail thing to have done, such a tiny change, and I am under no illusions about the impact my decision has made on the world. The answer is simple. On a global level, none. On a personal level, it rocked my world.

AFTER a few early-morning walks in the dark with Daisy the dog, a torch and my wellington boots, I'd had time to wonder if I'd decided to stop buying things because I felt guilty.

Guilty about what, though? Being a moderately successful person with enough money to live in a nice house, have enough to eat, stay warm in winter, wear nice clothes, drive new cars and go on long-haul holidays?

To a lot of people feeling guilty about these sorts of things doesn't make any sense. It's true it's a total waste of time, but I know I feel guilty.

I think it must be a very English, Anglo-Saxon and patently middle-class reaction which can afflict anyone from that subset who came of age before the Thatcher era. From what I can gather, people who were either at school during the Thatcher years or simply too young to even know who she was are not likewise afflicted.

There is a sector of the generations younger than me who seem to truly enjoy spending money on things they don't actually need. They wear and drive things that proclaim loudly to the world, 'I can spend a lot of money when I go out in the evening or drive along the road' and they seem to feel happy about it.

When I have enough money to do something mildly extravagant, I hesitate long and hard and if I do splash out I invariably feel guilty.

The first time I bought a brand-new car from a proper car showroom I was 43 years old. The car in question was a Volkswagen Golf VR6, dark green with leather seats, sparkly alloy wheels and low-profile tyres. Oh yes, ladies and gentleman, it was a seriously hot hatch.

As I lay in bed the first night I owned it, I writhed in regret. Seriously, I could not sleep. Up to that point I had only ever owned battered second-hand cars that cost very little money. This car cost quite a lot of money and I didn't casually purchase it as I wandered past the showroom one day. I had been dreaming about owning one for ages. I had read the reviews in the motoring pages of newspapers, I had watched the same model drive past in the street and strained my ears to hear the powerful Euro V6 throb coming from the twin tail pipes. I was hooked. I was the perfect consumer, being in the right place at the right time with a chequebook in my pocket.

However, my reaction on actually buying the car was exactly the opposite of the one the adverts and brochures had led me to expect. The advertising image of the confident man driving the powerful car had initially had the desired effect on me, but the experience of knowing this complex piece of machinery was sitting outside my house made me nothing but anxious. It was so new, so squeaky clean, and if I actually drove this amazing machine, it was going to get damaged, scratched, chipped, scraped and dirty. The roads around the rural area we live in are pitted and potholed, the lanes are very narrow, cars come the other way and there's not enough room to pass. The shock absorbers, so new and perfect, were going to get hammered. The sparkly magnesium alloy wheels would get chipped by the steep mud and gravel verges. The pristine interior was going to be ruined by the kids. It was a total nightmare.

I thrashed around, wondering if I could take it back to the dealer and trade it in for a pile-of-rubbish car that was already ten years old and pre-trashed. I knew this was stupid, but owning my new car made me anxious.

The next day, when I stared at it out of the kitchen window, my anxiety turned to guilt. There I was worrying about the well-being of a bloody car when there were millions of people in the world who didn't have enough to eat, had no electricity to cook or see by, had no medical facilities if they or their children became ill.

Not only that, but if they had the chance they would probably love to own something as smart as my car, and yet here I was, the new owner, and I felt like an idiot. I couldn't adjust my mindset to Thatcherite 'I deserve it, because I'm worth it' mode. Did I think I deserved to own an expensive car more than them? Simple answer: no.

And let me remind you, we are talking a Volkswagen here, not a Rolls-Royce or an Aston Martin. A bloody Golf with a bit of an up-market engine. I almost want to go back to the me of eight years ago just to say, 'Give yourself a break, you self-pitying pillock.'

But the guilt got worse. By now I felt guilty about feeling guilty. I was writhing in middle-class angst at being successful and having enough money to buy the damn thing. I also knew that the millions of people who couldn't afford it wouldn't necessarily be brimming with sympathy for the poor suffering liberal who could.

Here's a theory I've just come up with, based on nothing other than 52 years of life experience.

The Left (not a commonly used term any more) do shame, the Right (equally redundant) do guilt. Roman Catholics specialize in shame, Protestants adore guilt. Buddhists don't do either, while Muslims and Jews do both. Ooh, and while I'm on the topic, PC users do shame, while Mac users do guilt. That has to be so, because I am a Mac user (this is being written on a 24-inch iMac with 2 gigabytes of memory and a couple of terabytes of external storage) and I feel guilty about owning it, although I did buy it well before my year of not buying anything. Just to clarify that point, otherwise you might try to shame me.

PC users claim they don't think about what sort of computer they've bought, they just got the cheapest. But they know they are wrong and, when they see a Mac, they know they should have bought one of those. They are in the majority (93 per cent of computers on earth run Windows), which then makes them feel worse, because they haven't tried to be different, or they are too scared or ill informed to opt for an alternative. They hang their heads in shame as they endlessly wait for the clunking software it came with to reboot after it's been infected for the umpteenth time by some spamming 14-year-old hacker in Montenegro.

So guilt is not the same as shame. If you do something you feel guilty about in private, it makes no difference if no one else knows you are doing it; you can still feel guilty. Guilt comes from your internal voice, so the feeling of guilt comes from a process of self-criticism. You have a certain ideal of yourself and you fail to measure up to it. What you are striving to do when you deal with guilt is join together those two parts of yourself, the one that does something that makes you feel bad and the one that judges you.

When I think about it I get a little scared, because I am not normally aware of two 'me's living in my head. I have had a few mates who certainly did live with two 'me's inside them and they were very ill and spent a long time looking at a padded wall and dribbling. But when I do stop and think about it, when I haven't been shopping or looking at a magazine which tells me there is going to be an ultra-thin laptop coming out, I can understand that there is someone else, another voice, trying to push me to a more decent decision in all things. The voice that knows it is pointless to shout at the children when they leave the door open, the light on, the toilet unflushed, the single sock under the bed, the shoes not put away, the tap running, the wet towel on the floor ...

This is the voice that suggests the way we shop and the amount of rubbish we produce are wrong, driving cars with big engines is wrong, buying cheap clothes from the other side of the world is wrong. That voice, the gentle voice of reason and personal honesty, the caring voice which really doesn't sound anything like Jeremy Clarkson. That's the voice which makes the cheap, loud, brash bully in me stop in my tracks and feel guilty.

Now, from reading the relevant literature and laughing at various comedians, there seem to be two groups who truly understand and live with guilt and shame in a creative way. I'm talking Catholics and Jews. When I thought about this years ago, talked about it with my friends and even tried to write a stage play about it, I realized that most of my friends and lovers were either Catholics or Jews, although never both as far as I recall.

It's not like I hung around Catholic discos or Jewish restaurants in the hope of meeting them. It's simply the circles I mixed in, the places I worked and lived, the people I have been attracted to. Always Catholics and Jews. Oh yes, and homosexuals. Loads of them. But then most of the homosexuals I know are also either Catholic or Jewish, so let's stick with those primary groupings for a start.

I think it's important to point out that, as far as I know, there is no Jewish blood in my family and none of my relatives are or have been Catholic, so none of this attraction makes sense in any inherited genetic way.

What I do know is that Jews and Catholics are good at living with guilt and I am rubbish at it. I'm not very good at shame either and they are also good at that. They can criticize other people, i.e. shame them, sometimes with justification, and not feel any guilt about doing so. I live in a very fragile glass house – I'm talking metaphorically here, as I actually live in a wooden house, but the glass-house thing has always worked for me – I never throw stones. I fondle the odd metaphorical pebble, but I don't dare throw it.

Jews and Catholics seem to chuck rocks around without hesitation. They, too, live in glass houses, most of their windows are smashed or cracked and they don't seem to give a hoot. I have always felt they are having a whale of a time and it's not fair.

I have tried very hard to shrug off guilt, with little success. I just feel guilty about things regardless of what anyone else thinks or says.

A particular guilt-ridden event has stayed sharply in my memory for many years, from the period when my young and specifically male guilt reached a zenith of discomfort.

I was living in a student household in London in the mid-1970s and shared the small flat with three women and a blind man. We divided all the domestic tasks between us with Stalinist rigour. We talked late into the night, drinking tea and smoking cigarettes while we listened to J. J. Cale and Van Morrison on a battered stereo. We discussed Marxism, feminism and the Troops Out of Ireland movement, which was a very contentious issue at the height of the IRA London bombing campaign.

Two of the women were law students and both of them were involved in the creation of the UK's first rape crisis centre. Now, you don't need to be an expert in feminism or Marxist analysis to know what a rape crisis centre is. I heard many stories from these brave women that have stayed with me to this day.

So, as a white male heterosexual, all such dated terms now, there was plenty of potential guilt lying about. Oh yes, I had collected sack-loads of the stuff and I was only 19.

Guilt

In my small, almost-bare bedroom in this über-feminist, hyper-political environment, in my cupboard, under a box of old shoes, in the bottom corner right at the back, I can still see it now, burned into my memory even though the building has long since been demolished. Older men will know – at least 96 per cent of heterosexual males will know – what's under that box. Hidden, hopefully, from prying feminist eyes.

Yes, it was a glossy 'adult' magazine featuring many pictures of young ladies in various states of nudity. If any of the women I shared the house with had found that magazine, and this is the mid-1970s remember, very different times, I would have been publicly humiliated, thrown out of the house and expelled from my circle of friends without hesitation. I would have been shamed to the limits of human endurance, because I was seen by these women as a 'nice man' and a 'gentle man' and a 'caring non-sexist man who didn't use the C word all the time'.

That last bit is utterly true. The C word was an utter no-no, and I understood the reasoning behind it. This was a result of feminist consciousness-raising. Men used the C word as a derogatory term of abuse. I tried using the word here and I cut it out, because even now it makes me feel very uneasy. I can tell myself it's only a word, but it has such a violent resonance it is extraordinary. However, my peer group and I commonly used it when I was at school. It was a swearword, it was a very bad swearword, and that's why we liked using it. But when feminist women pulled me up on it, I listened and I understood their discomfort about me using it. I can honestly say that I never used the C word from early 1975 until some time around 1997. Not once, never. Amazing, isn't it?

In the 1970s it was fully accepted in my circles that all men were rapists and all pornography was rape in picture form. Fair enough, I could see the point. Not only could I see it, I agreed with it wholeheartedly, but I still had a girlie mag hidden in my cupboard, and the guilt – I cannot tell you the fear and dread I experienced.

An event occurred during this period which racked up the guilt and overhanging shame to quite an absurd degree. During the hot summer of 1975 there was an international feminist conference in London. Women from all over the world gathered to talk – I don't know what about, obviously, as I wasn't there; men weren't allowed to attend. But while all these women from overseas were in London they needed to stay somewhere. Twenty-two women from the Lotta Continua (the Struggle Continues) movement in Italy stayed with us. Twenty-two young Italian women in a small four-bedroomed flat. Eight of them stayed in my room, dossing on the floor.

It's hard to imagine now, even for me, but that's what happened. They unrolled their sleeping bags on the floor while I cleared my stuff into one corner. None of them spoke English and I didn't speak Italian. I didn't even dare smile at them and I'll tell you why.

Unreconstructed men might already be having some sort of *Playboy*-style fantasy about eight young Italian women staying in their bedroom when they were 19 years old. However, before these women arrived I had discovered that quite a few of them had recently been arrested in Rome while they were demonstrating outside a police station. They were demonstrating because a 14-year-old girl had been raped by a family member and went to the police station to report it, where she was promptly raped again by three police officers in a cell. For fairly obvious reasons, these young women were not a bag of laughs or up for some kinky international hanky-panky with a scrawny long-haired Brit.

Add to that, I had a girlie mag in my cupboard, only inches away from a sleeping Italian feminist. The stress I felt cannot be exaggerated. My heart was pounding and I didn't sleep a wink. As soon as one of them moved I tensed up, convinced she was going to open the cupboard, lift the box of shoes and start a riot.

Thankfully, this didn't happen and I eventually smuggled the offending pornography out of the house and deposited it in a litter bin on the Euston Road, still nervous that someone would see me doing it. In fact, as far as I know, none of the women I shared that flat with ever knew I had it, so we are clearly talking guilt here, not shame.

I was terrified of being humiliated, exposed and criticized as well. But that wasn't enough to stop me doing it, and if anything these fears made the wretched magazine all the more attractive.

What really got to me was that I also felt guilty about it even after I had thrown it away. There was a better man inside me trying to make himself heard, someone who understood that while I found the image of the naked female form attractive for entirely benign and biological reasons, I also knew that a complex and detrimental system of exploitation was taking place in order for me to be able to see the naked women and I didn't want to be part of that.

And that is the clue that helped me. I decided that if I didn't buy pornographic magazines, then in a small way I was helping to undermine the system that created them, the system that made it OK for women to be exploited by the publishing companies that produced them. It removed the guilt and shame from my life and allowed me to walk down the street, past feminists, and not leave the pungent waft of porn guilt in my wake. I can remember moments like that, when I would turn up at events and actually think to myself, 'I don't have any porn hidden anywhere, I have nothing to feel shame about, I am free.'

It makes me laugh now. And of course that feeling was only very occasional. It was normally, 'Oh, my God, I hope they don't find the massive pile of hardcore filth under the bed.'

Guilt and shame never stopped me for long, therefore, when I gave up buying things for a year. I knew from long experience that they would not be enough to help me get through.

As an interesting side note, I experienced a piquant guilt twist as I sat writing this. I live about 100 miles outside London and wrote part of the chapter on a very crowded commuter train on my way home. I was travelling first-class because it provides me with room to write on my laptop during the rush hour, a thing I normally try to avoid. (Obviously, I couldn't buy a newspaper or a magazine during this year of not shopping, and I wasn't carrying one of the previous year's unread books with me, but if you go first-class they give you a free newspaper. See the chapter on cheating, page 157.)

The fact that I can choose to travel on a first-class ticket also means I can afford a first-class ticket, which makes me feel mildly guilty. However, on this particular journey the train was packed, standing room only for a lot of surprisingly cheery British travellers used to such hardship. They were standing throughout the train, including in the first-class carriage. I had a big comfy seat and just stared fixedly at my keyboard and typed, hoping no one would look at me and suggest I offer them my seat. As the journey progressed and the crowd thinned, between the seats in front of me I could see a very smartly dressed woman in late middle age who was wearing a lot of make-up. I mean a lot. I don't want to judge her for wearing a lot of make-up; I might have a strong desire to explain to her that some people find that level of heavy make-up worrying or even frightening, but I would never say anything.

When the ticket inspector finally made it through the crush she berated him on the fact that she had paid a lot of money for an exclusive first-class ticket (that's how she described it), only to find herself in a carriage crowded with lanky students on ultra-cheap student rail cards who were on their way back to Oxford. The poor ticket inspector, a charming man with a strong Worcestershire accent, tried to jolly her along, saying he understood how she felt but there was nothing he could do. She shook her head as he spoke, constantly repeating that she had bought the aforementioned exclusive first-class ticket and she wasn't getting exclusive first-class service.

Now, I couldn't do that. I admit that it did occur to me that I had also paid a lot of money for my exclusive first-class ticket and I had a man sitting next to me who couldn't believe his luck. He told me he had a cheap-day super-saver return but he knew the guard would never be able to get through the packed carriage to check. He got off at Oxford, which is why I am free to write this now, as I have the feeling he was having a sneaky read as I was writing about guilt, something he clearly wasn't experiencing.

But I am ashamed about any privileged position I find myself in. This might be because I spent long enough with zero privileges and even less money to clearly remember what it's like to look in from the outside. Or, of course, it might be because of my mum.

'Grabbed my watch off my dresser this morning, dropped it, swore, picked it up, checked it, not ticking, just making grating loose-part noises. I will have to get it repaired. I love my watch, I've had it for years and it's only the beginning of January. More swearing.'

HERE'S a little bit of shame and probably a bit of guilt too. I made my decision to stop shopping on 23 December while on a solitary walk. What I haven't fully explained is that I was walking barefoot along a beach. The observant reader will have picked up a clue there. What northern European would walk barefoot along a beach in December? I might be a bit of a sackcloth-and-ashes merchant but I couldn't do that ... I have very sensitive feet.

I was, in fact, walking along a beautiful hot beach in Australia, which can only mean that I had flown there from

England, just before Christmas.

When you see adverts on the side of a bus for flights to Australia for a few hundred pounds, let me assure you that these are not the direct flights you need to book many months in advance in order to fly there just before Christmas. Any backpacker on a budget will know that this is not a good time to fly to the Antipodes. The price goes off the scale as the airlines make as much money as possible from people returning to see their families for Christmas.

The reason I was in Australia was because I am the Anglo part of an Anglo-Australian marriage, the type of liaison that should be strongly discouraged in the lonely hearts section of any eco-friendly publication worthy of the title.

Caring, sensitive English eco male WLTM Australian eco woman, GSOH. Interests: cycling, organic gardening, solar energy, multiple long-haul flights.

In the past 20 years I have flown to Australia something like 16 times. That's a lot of air miles, that's a pretty chunky carbon footprint, and of course it has created even more guilt. When our children were little pre-school angels of joy we'd spend months at a time there. It was irresistible to be able to miss the worst bit of the UK winter. Don't get me wrong. Many's the time I would be sitting writing in the shade of a beachside house as my children frolicked in a crystal-clear pool with their mum and cousins and I would smile to myself in deep self-congratulatory satisfaction. It would be mid-January and I'd try to picture the cold and dark back home. Obviously I always felt a little bit shameful about it. Not just the carbon-footprint issue; I felt shame because I could afford to go and stay there for such an extended period and I felt the need to justify it to my friends and colleagues. I would explain that although it's expensive to get there, once we were there it was very cheap, and anyway I was working.

How stupid is that?

I have tried to work out where that guilt comes from. No one I knew was saying to me, 'Oh, look at you, spending three months on a beach writing a novel while we slog it out on the commuter run every day.' They either didn't care or said the British equivalent of 'G'donyer, mate.'

It's that awkward feeling which is the curse of the overprivileged liberal and makes the Jeremy Clarkson-style reactionary stance so darned attractive. I have tried that attitude on for size and it just didn't work for me. I don't want to be a rich person living in a poor world. I don't want to drive a big flash car in the rain past poor cold people waiting for a bus. I can't be comfortable in the knowledge that I deserve the privilege because I have worked very hard for it.

I've had many good-hearted friends try to encourage me to accept my position with good grace. 'You've worked very hard for your money. It's fine. Enjoy it.'

They are right, of course. It is actually unforgivable to be in my position and feel shameful about it. And guess what? I feel guilty about that.

I am married to a Catholic (profoundly lapsed) who doesn't suffer from guilt very much at all and only does shame as an occasional hobby. I should have picked up a few tips over the last 20 years, but I haven't and I feel guilty about that, too. Maybe that's the point I'm missing. I have always assumed that Catholics and Jews are riddled with guilt because they tend to discuss it a great deal, but in fact they simply understand guilt and shame much better than an uptight Proddy like me and don't lug it around with them all the time.

So there I was in Australia, walking along the beautiful beach early in the morning, feeling slightly shameful as always. I was trying to come up with ways of sloughing that particular skin. It was a couple of days before Christmas and we had just been on a monster shopping trip.

My wife's family in Australia is quite a size. She has three brothers and two of them have three children. Then there's grandma, aunts and uncles, various distant cousins, in-laws, in-laws' children and so on. The Christmas gathering has been enormous in the past, so the amount of presents can build up. Of course, our kids love it. It's the part of the family they rarely see and there are plenty of cousins the same age as them. It's hot, they have swimming pools to frolic in, the beach is down the road, there are weird insects to look at – they have a blast.

The shopping trip we had been on the day before the beach walk was long and arduous, and when faced with such plenty, I go into a haze of indecision. I am overwhelmed by the choice and abundance of consumer goods, my head hurts with the colours, the special offers, the helpful shop assistants, the racks of clothing in different sizes, the music, the lighting. To me, a shopping mall is a living hell.

For someone to make a decision not to buy anything for himself after such an event doesn't quite make sense. I wasn't buying anything for myself at all, I was busy buying things for other people, my extended Australian family, which obviously makes me feel more guilty for begrudging the shopping excursion.

There is a complex family tradition with my in-laws that I very willingly engage in. Early in the year they draw up a list that results in every adult family member buying one present for another adult member of the family. The kids end up with loads, but we adults get one present each. It's a beautiful compromise that doesn't deny the institution but keeps it manageable. It is eminently sensible.

So I only had to buy one gift for my brother-in-law. However, the combined experience of buying stuff for my children and their six Australian cousins was still amazingly complex and, for me, highly stressful. They are no longer delightful little children who might appreciate an inexpensive new toy or a sweet cuddly teddy. They are all approaching their teens and they want clothes, bikes, skateboards, trainers, iPods, mobile phones, their own Amazon account, motorbikes, trust funds, a private jet and an apartment in New York. You know, normal run-of-the-mill stuff.

I don't want to make out my family to be a bunch of avaricious consumer junkies, because they're really not. But they all seemed to thoroughly enjoy themselves that day and were keen to find things to give each other. It's far more likely that I am an old Scrooge, a term my son enjoyed using to describe me when I moaned about him needing yet another pair of skate shoes.

I think my response was very much linked to my children. If I see them playing in the sand, running along a beach, giggling with their friends, throwing a stick for our dog, I feel happy, complete, nurturing and wise.

If I watch them pawing through Chinese-made clothes in an overpriced, label-obsessed surf store on Australia's Gold Coast, I feel alienated, powerless, depressed, anxious and slightly grumpy.

That was one side of it. The other side was pure guilt at an unfocused combination of talent, diligence, skill and pure, as I often see it, undeserved luck which had allowed me to be there to observe them. I was standing in this massive store watching my children consume because I could afford to be there. I could afford to let my children buy stuff there, we could afford to rent the apartment we had near the beach and hire the enormous car we had parked in the multi-storey. I felt guilty simply because I earned more than the national average. I felt guilty because we have a large house in the country and a tiny flat in the middle of London. I felt guilty because we have three cars and an Aga cooker.

In one very financially successful year in the late 1990s I was paid far more than my father earned in his entire working life. I took the time to work it out and he was very much on my mind as he had just died a few months before. I can honestly say that during this particular year I was the most anxious and miserable I have ever been. I felt a huge burden of responsibility.

But you keep busy and bury the anxieties in the hectic logistics of life, consumerism, international travel and gift-buying.

So there I was in the sun-soaked mall and there was nothing I could do about it: it was too late, I was too powerless, I had no control over things. Making a big fuss and demanding that all the children stop buying anything would have been overly dramatic, even for me, and I love a bit of drama.

So after a day like that the prospect of avoiding such a place for a whole year was positively exciting. Giving up buying new things for a year didn't fill me with dread; it was more like a glimmer of hope in an otherwise bleak universe. I wanted to stop feeling guilty and I was looking for a way of doing so. It was going to be interesting to see if it worked.

Giving Up

FEB
17
2007

'Spent ages doing a stocktake of my clothes. It was
a pretty depressing exercise, I have such a drab
collection of worn-out stuff. I've been making do for
years, there's nothing new in my possession. How is
any of this collection of rags going to last me all year?
I dug through an old box of stuff I was going to take
to a charity shop and decided to reintroduce it to
my day-to-day wardrobe. By cutting up a pair of old
baggy shorts I never wore much, I patched some
favourite old trousers and proudly showed them to
Judy. She was not impressed, implying that it was high
time I got over having been a hippie 30 years ago. She
may have a point.'

I HAVE to admit that in the whole giving-up-shopping debate
I am at a huge advantage. I have given up so many things over

the last 50 years I have a wealth of experience. I used this to bolster myself in the early months of the year.

In our youth we can't wait to take things up – to be old enough to smoke, drink, take illegal drugs, drive and have sex – but once you're past your mid-thirties, life is all about giving things up.

There are millions of people giving things up all the time. Drink, drugs, cigarettes, meat, sex, religion, nail-biting, looking at porn, eating too much, buying new things ... The list goes on and on. Giving things up and presumably trying to feel better about yourself as a result are nothing short of an epidemic in the developed world.

I know I have given up just about everything in the above list and a few other unmentionable habits besides. Not illegal ones involving the abuse of other people, but unpleasant things like speaking with your mouth full. I accept that in the grand scheme of crimes against humanity, that one probably doesn't rank very high. I imagine that if Pol Pot had been talking while eating a bowl of rice, none of his mates would have said, 'Hey, Pol, please don't speak with your mouth full, mate. It's well gross.' But it is a bad habit of mine when dining with friends. It is utterly unforgivable to spray your mates with half-chewed salad when you get excited about a subject.

With some of the things I've given up I've been gloriously successful. It wasn't hard and I've never thought about it since. Other activities have been a lifelong struggle.

However, at one time or another I've secretly done all the things I'd claimed to have given up. I'd try to hide the fact from other people but, more importantly, I'd lie to myself to help the conceit.

A good example I sometimes use to remind myself of my inner cheating is when I fell hopelessly in love (for a short time, I was young) with a committed vegan called Sue. This was back in the early 1970s and Sue was a beautiful, willowy blonde hippie girl who consumed absolutely no animal products in any form and washed her skin with cider vinegar. That last bit was fairly confusing. I got the whole no-meat thing, that was easy to understand, but the cider vinegar ... It's a smell I still associate with her to this day and not a product I can easily use in my culinary creations.

I have Googled cider vinegar and obviously there are plenty of people who believe it has amazing medicinal qualities, but that's when you take three drops in a glass of water. I never truly understood why Sue washed with it. I suppose it was to do with not using soap, which generally contains tallow, an animal fat. You can actually make your own soap from pig fat, as I know because I've actually done it on a TV show.

Anyway, Sue the vegan said she loved me but wouldn't even kiss me because I ate meat, which was true but still fairly harsh. Not only did I eat meat but, being strongly influenced by a kind of medievalist ethos springing from the movies of Pasolini, in particular *The Canterbury Tales* and *The Decameron*, I occasionally hunted for meat with a bow and arrow.

Does that sound weird? I suppose it was. I was under 20, so give me a break.

I only hunted rabbits. Often in the early morning I could be found out in the fields with my longbow, shooting bunnies. Obviously I never told Sue the vegan about my hunting habits and because I had met my dream medieval princess I knew I would have to stop eating meat.

I hung up my bow and quiver of arrows and for about two weeks I really did stop. I didn't cheat once. I became a total vegetarian. I managed to convince her that I was heading towards complete veganism but I was doing it in stages. I was still using milk in my tea, eating eggs and using butter on bread. She accepted that and kissed me. It was worth it. That kiss made me feel I could be a vegetarian for a long time and I felt better for it.

On Sue's advice, and believe me she had plenty of that, I went on a weird macrobiotic cleansing diet. Now, I think it's important to explain that a diet wasn't something I really needed at the time. When I was 19 years old I don't know how I had the muscular strength to stand up; I was a human stick insect. The cleansing diet consisted of organic brown rice and water, as much and as often as you wanted. I could eat a bucketful of brown rice if I felt like it and drink gallons of water. The water I could do, but the rice, that was a toughie. We're not talking raw brown rice here, that would be ridiculous, although I bet some hippie hermit from California has had a go. This was cooked brown rice, no salt, no seasoning, just plain, plain, plain. I sometimes managed a small bowl and that was it. I hated the damn stuff, but I was becoming cleansed of all the toxins I had accumulated from years of bad eating. That's how it was sold to me by Sue the vegan.

Obviously, this sort of change in your life has a fairly profound effect. On a physical level it left me feeling very light-headed. As for an inner-peace, spiritual-journey kind of experience, well, I suppose it was almost spiritual, but with me any experience is only ever almost spiritual, it's never actually spiritual.

However, to me the most shocking thing was that for the first time in my life I had spots, like a proper adolescent. Great buboes all over my face – something I'd never suffered previously. They really hurt, don't they? I showed them to Sue the vegan and out came the cider vinegar to cleanse them. Oh yes, let me tell you, cider vinegar dabbed on an angry boil, that takes you into a whole new world of pain.

About three weeks into the project I was walking back to the house we lived in, a squat on the edge of Bath. It's true, this took place in the glorious and ancient Roman spa town of Aquae Sulis, a world-renowned beauty spot, so no scruffy terraced derelict; this was a dead posh Georgian mansion. To me in my heightened brown-rice-and-water distorted mental state, it was a medieval banqueting hall with a drawbridge and a moat.

I was walking home alone. It was dark and very likely to have been raining, which is never a good thing when you are wearing hand-made medieval-style shoes and a thin jerkin made of some cloth that absorbs water like a sponge. I would imagine I had a cold, as I was constantly unhealthy during this period. On my way through the dark murky night I passed a fish and chip shop. The smell, which I would normally find mildly nauseating, was suddenly intensely, headily, insatiably appealing. I smelt high-fat cooking oil, chips, crisp golden batter and vinegar; malt vinegar with chemicals, not organic cider vinegar in an earthenware jar. The heady waft that escaped from the doors of this pre-extractor-fan chippery drove me crazy. I glanced up and down the street for prying vegan eyes, then, without further hesitation, dived inside.

This was the only time in my life that I have actually had a sausage fritter. Normally I wouldn't dream of eating such a dubiously sourced meat product, but I devoured it with a passion normally reserved for actors who are pretending they haven't seen food for a week. Of course, immediately I finished this battered delight I felt like a heel. I was really trying to be a vegan and be all pure and healthy. I wanted to do it over and above my desire for the medieval elfin princess who, as I wiped my mouth on my medieval sleeve, would be bathing her beauty in cider vinegar, awaiting the return of her knight.

I bought a packet of mints from a newsagent's and tried to cover the sin that lingered on my breath. As far as I recall, Sue never said anything about it; if she noticed she didn't comment. But a rough-hewn part-time medievalist such as myself was never going to be compatible with a fully-fledged princess like Sue. Pretty soon I was cooking hand-killed rabbit and she went off to live in a bender in the Black Mountains. That's what people did in those days; it was nothing to be concerned about.

But that's just giving up meat: easy-peasy. What about tobacco? Now that's a real burden. I gave up smoking in January 1990. It wasn't easy but I did it. No pills, patches, gum, hypnosis or group support. I used my fairly unique method of getting through the first few days, and from casual conversations with other people who've given up smoking, it's not something that the NHS helpline suggests. I think they should, because it definitely works.

I called it the 'scream, bathe and masturbate' method. Whenever you want a cigarette you do any or all of the above, any number of times a day. There were days when I had six or seven baths, screamed until I was utterly voiceless and obviously masturbated like a Trojan. I have no historical proof that Trojans masturbated with more than the usual masculine vigour, but they just sound like the sort of blokes who would knock one out with a particularly manly roar. There you are, passing through the Troas Mountains during Trojan times, and you hear this amazing sound echoing down the valley. You turn to your travelling companion and say, 'Whoa, that was a biggie. Must have been a Trojan beating the bishop.'

I was lucky at the time. When I gave up puffing this oddly legal and most addictive weed I had a small utility room in my rented flat which was fairly isolated from the rest of the building, so I presumed I wouldn't disturb my neighbours too much – that was for the screaming, obviously. When you scream and scream you hyperventilate, which makes you a bit high. You need to lie down and rest afterwards, then I'd bathe again, and then the rest of it. I'll spare you the details, but let's just say I didn't get a lot of writing done. The withdrawals only lasted three days and I was done with fags, but by that time I was utterly voiceless, surgical-instrument clean and rather sore in the nether regions. Once it was over I didn't think about it any more and didn't cheat once. I'm very proud to say I fathered two children as a total non-smoker; cigarettes and babies really don't go together.

Everything was fine in the whole nicotine-addict area in my life until, in the late 1990s, I discovered that my father had lung cancer. Well, I didn't discover it – 'Father, I've looked at your

X-rays and I'm afraid I have bad news.' No, a doctor found out after my dad had a fall on the tennis court. He played regularly into his mid-seventies and, like most men, never went to the doctor. It was only this fall and the resultant pain he was in that finally forced him to seek the advice of a 'quack', as he would have referred to a doctor.

The doctor eventually told the family. He explained our dad had probably had cancer for years but because of his age it was fairly stable. Although my dad had given up smoking a good 15 years before he died, he used to seriously chain it and I would imagine he started smoking during the war. He was an RAF navigator and pilot and I believe they were actually given cigarettes as part of their rations. Ahh, the good old days.

I know my dad hated giving things up; it made him grumpy and miserable. When he stopped smoking he put on weight, and I mean a lot of weight. There is no denying it, my dad was a very sizeable gentleman. When he was the same age as I am now he weighed over 5 stone more than I do and I'm a bit of a lump. He was advised to go on a diet, which really annoyed him. 'Blasted namby-pamby do-gooders' would be a very good guess at his reaction to the suggestion.

He had to give up dairy products and red meat, so he ate fruit, by the box-load. From what I can gather about the intimacies between my parents, he'd given up all hope of having sex not long after my sister was born, so that wasn't an option. Then he gave up work, because in most industries you have to retire whether you want to or not, but it wasn't until he gave up tennis and gardening due to the fall that he finally gave up life.

I can see now that I was lucky I had time to spend with my father just before he died. Whatever the reasons for his demise at that particular point in time, it felt like he had chosen his moment well, for me at least. I wasn't in Australia with my family or halfway through a recording of a TV series with an intense life-absorbing schedule, so I was able to visit him in hospital in Oxford on a regular basis.

It is not an exaggeration to say that my father and I didn't really see eye to eye for most of my adult life, although all my early childhood memories of him are very happy ones. It would be fair to classify him as being on the extreme right of the political spectrum; he thought Margaret Thatcher was a bit of a sell-out liberal. For him, the *Daily Mail* was a wishy-washy middle-of-the-road kind of paper, so having a son like me can never have been easy.

As he lay on his deathbed, we talked and laughed and joked in the slightly cruel way my family has always had. On one particularly memorable day during this time I woke up early, bathed and dressed my two-year-old daughter, then drove to the NHS hospital (where, I want to point out, he was looked after with angelic care). I was told by the nurses that he was about to have a bed bath. I asked Dad if I could help and he said he didn't mind, so I helped flannel-wash my old man.

It was absurdly symbolic. Being the blabbermouth I am and to relieve the tension I was feeling (I was born in the 1950s, this was the first time I had ever seen my father naked), I told him my theory on how we have to let others care for us at the beginning and end of life. When we put him back into his bed he told me I had always been a f*****g idiot but he was proud of me.

That was the first time he had ever said anything like that to me. Never before had he asked me what I was doing or how life was going. He showed virtually no interest in anything I did and I can see now that I spent my entire life trying to prove to him that I was not gay, as he always suggested, and that some of my ideas might have some validity.

With that one simple comment, guarded by a joke and a swearword, he released me from a life of anger and regret about him. He died two days later, with enormous dignity and bravery, and utterly changed my view of him, allowing me to let go of the bitterness I had previously felt towards him.

It had to be at least six months after he died that I was standing with my sister in a garden at some sort of family gathering and we were both smoking. My sister hadn't smoked for 22 years, yet as soon as our dad died due to smoking-related cancer we both started again. We came up with various theories about why we did so, but none of them truly made sense. There is certainly something about the death of a parent that means in the grand scheme of things you are next on the list. I suppose this could mean some voice inside me went, 'Oh well, you are going to kick the bucket soon enough. Might as well light up and enjoy the last few years.'

From that point on I have been fighting a constant rearguard action, sometimes stopping for months at a time, only to start again during a moment of stress.

I am not smoking now as I write this, but I know myself well enough to know I might be next week, next month or next year.

Giving up shopping and buying new stuff has been absurdly easy in comparison. It may be because I set myself the goal of only doing it for a year. If I did that with smoking I could manage it.

Idea for a book, *Fagged Out: A Year of Not Smoking* by Robert Llewellyn. Mmmm, could sell.

When I don't smoke I dream of being in a smoky pub with my friends and fagging on like a 1950s squaddie. Thankfully, the smoky-pub location is no longer an option, but if I see a picture of the superbly ravaged face of the poet W. H. Auden with a fag hanging out of his mouth, I want to be like him. I find such images doomed, romantic and appealing, whereas the image of someone walking through a shopping mall loaded down with massive carrier bags full of non-essential consumer goods seems utterly unappealing.

However you look at it, it's pretty obvious we consume too much, be it food, cigarettes, cars, computers or clothes. We truly don't need a third of what we buy and yet our world is constructed around us continuing to do so. And that is a much bigger problem. It is painfully obvious to me now, and I mean painfully, because despite appearances I'm not looking forward to it, that people in the developed world are going to have to get used to giving up quite a lot of things. And not just for a year, but for good.

'For some obscure reason I always recall my 22nd birthday when I wake up on this day. Only because this day is my birthday, I don't think about it any other time. It was anything but remarkable. I went for an early-morning walk in Oxfordshire, where I was living at the time. I knew I was about to move to London and I knew I would miss the wilder parts of the world where I had spent so much time up until then. During the walk I stopped in some dense woodland and squatted down, looking through the trees as my dog, a scruffy mongrel called Ruffage, went snuffling through the undergrowth.

I think I may have genuinely experienced some inner calm and peace at that moment, as it has stayed with me in such sharp focus. The weak winter sun coming through the leafless trees, the air crisp, cold but fresh. It quite simply felt good to be alive.

My 51st birthday has had little of that charm. It's fallen on a Saturday and I'm at home. My daughter, Holly, has been poorly and is slowly getting better. Judy gave me a pair of new underpants and then I had to get the children to their various activities. I don't think I stopped for a moment to sniff the air, reflect on my life. Shame really, but that's just the way it is. I did take the dog out for a walk early in the morning and that is the only time I truly get to reflect on anything amid the pandemonium of family life.

However, having a birthday at the end of winter has always put a spring in my step. Got this far, let's see what the year really brings. It's when I seem to stop worrying about the plight of the planet, when the buds start to show, the snowdrops re-emerge from the cold earth. Somehow even with all the damage we've done to the place, the earth seems to recover and move on.

At least that's what we are all beginning to hope.'

IT WOULD appear the whole eco-awareness movement as we know it today only truly started in the late 1960s, when the human race first saw the truly wonderful pictures of our stunning planet taken through the window of a space capsule on its way to the moon.

These pictures had a much bigger impact on me than the blurred black-and-white images of a man on the moon. For a start they were fantastically clear, taken with a high-resolution still camera, not a fairly rubbish 1960s black-and-white video camera. It was the smallness of our planet, its isolation in space, the fragility of this soft, blue-green sphere that really struck me.

I was 13 when the Apollo spacecraft landed on the moon and that, as we know, is a very impressionable age. Certainly many people my age were inspired by this event and wanted to become astronauts. Not me. I didn't want to go into space, because all the astronauts I saw on the TV were shaven-headed soldiers and I wanted to have long hair, wear elven clothes and live in a Hobbit hole. But the image of the planet never left me.

Also I soon found out, to my delight, that I wasn't alone in these feelings. There was a wonderful book published in the early 1970s called *The Whole Earth Catalogue*, which featured this image on its cover. I suppose the image said to all of us, 'This is it, people, this small blue-green globe floating in the unimaginable vastness of space is all we have and we'd better start looking after it.'

The Whole Earth Catalogue wasn't some miserable, downbeat, mealy-mouthed and pious approach to ecological awareness and action. It had that totally American, new world, 'there's still hope if we work at this together' type of attitude. It was playful, optimistic, revolutionary maybe, but not in a violent way. It merely suggested an alternative to the headlong dash into mass consumerism that was truly gearing itself up by this stage. There was a farewell message on the last page of the catalogue. It said, 'Stay hungry, stay foolish,' a bit of advice I have tried with varying degrees of success to follow.

Not surprisingly, many of the people involved in producing *The Whole Earth Catalogue* went on to help create the very early versions of resource pages on the Internet. The publication was essentially a paperback version of Google, as comprehensive a list as could possibly be packed inside its large-format pages. I eagerly consumed page after page of information about tools and resources for people trying to find alternative ways of living, a very popular idea in those times. I loved thumbing through it and it made me think about the world I lived in more than anything else I read at that time.

During the same period I read an intriguing book by the scientist and philosopher (Richard) Buckminster Fuller called *Approaching the Benign Environment*, which put forward the argument that we could invent our way out of global catastrophe with new technologies and radical approaches to the problems of climate change, overpopulation and waste management. One of the nuttier suggestions was that we should dispose of our most toxic waste in deep space: just shoot it out of the atmosphere and forget about it. Now, I'm no physicist and correct me if I'm wrong, but if we are floating around on this blue-green blob, it strikes me that by definition we must have finite resources we can use. Everything we have made on this planet comes from this planet. If we shoot all our rubbish out into space the world is going to steadily get smaller and smaller, isn't it? It just didn't strike my 13-year-old brain as a realistic solution. Plus, if we use a fleet of space shuttles as global garbage trucks, I imagine the average council tax bill is going to get hoicked up a bit.

Much of this philosophy and thought has faded from my everyday life now I have two children and two mortgages. In some ways, as an interest in ethical living and recycling has become the accepted norm, I have grown more blasé about it. I've been aware of these issues my entire adult life and also realize that even though I have always been careful with my garbage and hate the amount of stuff I throw away, as an individual I am pretty powerless. It's very easy to fall into a state of complacency because finally, after years of hectoring, corporations are now telling us they are doing something about it. Suddenly they have ethical and green policies, and profess to care about the world we live in. Yeah, right ...

Thoughts like these only really started flooding back into my life during the year I didn't buy anything new. It made me stop and think about ethical living all over again, after nearly 30 years when those sorts of ideas were just niggling worries somewhere at the back of my mind. Imagine for a moment if everyone on earth gave up buying anything new for one specific, prearranged year – when they reached the age of 43, or something random like that. First, it's important to remember that it would make no discernible difference to a huge percentage of the global population who don't have the resources to buy anything new anyway, so they wouldn't notice any difference other than the drop in sales of the T-shirts or shoes they manufacture for less than a dollar a day.

The rest of us, though, would surely notice rather a lot.

Since my early teens I have been in awe of the sheer scale of mass production around the world. This may be due to the fact that I spent the first few years of my working life manufacturing things by hand. The absurdity of this now leaves me baffled.

There I was, growing up in an advanced economy where people had struggled, invented, devised and created amazing machinery to produce goods with the minimal amount of manual intervention, and I was part of a sizeable movement on the fringe which was dedicated to stepping back in time and creating things individually, using only manual labour.

In my case I made shoes, bespoke shoes, the irony of course being that they were bought exclusively by very wealthy customers. I did an apprenticeship at a company called James Taylor's just off London's Marylebone High Street. The shop is still there if you want to see what a shop looks like that hasn't changed one tiny bit since 1975. At the time they made mainly orthopaedic shoes for people with physical disabilities; it's something you see far less of now, due to advances in surgery, but back then there were people with some very odd feet knocking about.

I then went on to be an outworker for John Lobb, that's the royal shoemaker, whose very exclusive shop is on St James's Street, just around the corner from St James's Palace. You know those massive black boots the Horse Guards wear that come up over the knee at the front? Lobb's make those. You know the riding boots Prince Charles wears when he plays polo? Lobb's. The shoes the Queen wears when she takes the corgis out at Balmoral? Yes, Lobb's. When Churchill made his V-for-victory sign he was wearing Lobb's. And James Bond – Lobb's.

The cavernous basement of John Lobb's contains the lasts, the wooden moulds the shoes are constructed on, of many thousands of people. I sometimes wandered through the racks of shelving which housed them as I ate my lunch. I found Winston Churchill's lasts, and Charlie Chaplin's, but never James Bond's. Maybe MI6 keep those.

If I worked flat out all week, I could just about produce four pairs of gentlemen's brogues. At the same time I went round a shoe factory in Northampton, and this was a posh shoe factory that produced the machine-made equivalent of what I would spend my day sweating over. In that factory one man could produce four pairs in about 20 minutes.

I didn't stop making shoes because of this. I stopped because I accidentally fell on a stage, accidentally made people laugh, accidentally ended up in a theatre group which toured for five years, accidentally became a stand-up comic and playwright, then accidentally ended up in a BBC sitcom which ran for ten years, which was swiftly and equally accidentally followed by presenting an engineering game show for ten more years.

All through this semi-career I would occasionally stare at things for no other reason than to try and understand the scale of the industry that produced them. Things like cars, street furniture, door handles, televisions, ships, planes, bridges, fridges, cat flaps, dining-room tables and central-heating radiators.

The incredible number of factories that produce an overwhelming collection of things, the roads that connect these factories, the ships and container systems that move them across the globe, the speed at which they have been developed. I am fascinated by the complexity of distribution systems, the fact that the man in the van who does the last mile of delivery to the shop or our front doors is part of a massive, complex network that someone, somewhere has worked out. I am confounded to the point of inactivity by the numbers of people who buy things and where all these things are before people buy them. I am still in awe at the ever-increasing rate of newness, of the latest thing, the bigger, faster, better thing.

I am also frightened by the size of the organizations that do all this. Even in my lifetime they have grown from being merely very big, where no one person could possibly control them, to so overbearingly gargantuan that no single country can control them, let alone a mere individual.

I know I am not alone in this dizzying confusion. I suppose it's possible that I find it hard to understand and become engaged with because of my attraction to the alternative view that was prominently on offer in my youth.

A philosopher and economist called E. F. Schumacher wrote a very popular book called *Small is Beautiful*, which was a best-seller in the 1970s. It's available on Amazon, I checked, or you could order it at a library if you're not buying anything for a year. I believe it's still very much worth reading.

Old Professor Schumacher had a very simple solution to the massive uncontrollable economic world we find ourselves living in, though unfortunately it's not one I can ever envisage being widely adopted. His basic premise was that small manufacturing entities are easier to control and have a less damaging global impact than large ones. He also thought that small villages and small towns were easier to live in than mega cities. One thing that struck me as a young man was his simple image of two trucks driving along a motorway in the UK. The first was carrying a type of English biscuit from the south of England all the way to Scotland; the second was carrying Scottish biscuits all the way from Scotland to the south of England. He gently suggested this might not be the best way to operate, and clearly he has a point, but then I have just suggested you buy his book from Amazon, which will no doubt entail a truck driving from Amazon's main distribution depot, which is near Milton Keynes, I believe, to a post office sorting centre somewhere, where it will be put on another truck to a local post office, where it will be put in a van and finally your postal worker will pop it through the letter box. (Notice I didn't say postman – see, I grew up in the 1970s.)

It's the world we live in and we have all got used to it, but that doesn't mean we shouldn't question it at every opportunity. I have to bear in mind that questioning it too much might mean no shortbread biscuits with tartan wrappers in the Southampton Waitrose and no custard creams in the Glasgow Budgens.

This is the problem we are all faced with: the more we know, the more information we have in our grasp, the bigger and more complex the problems we are faced with. When someone in our village fails to mow the grass in the churchyard (yes, that was me, my name was on the rota and I forgot), the issue is small, local, easy to manage, just as Professor Schumacher postulated. So is there anything we can really do about the big stuff?

I wonder what sort of effect, say, ten million people in the developed world who did consume a great deal normally and then suddenly stopped buying anything new for a year would have on the global economy. You don't need a degree in economics to work out it would be pretty catastrophic.

It wouldn't affect only manufacturing industries, but retail, the media, banking, distribution, advertising; the whole lot would be shaken to their very foundations.

It's the kind of fantasy I had when I was an adolescent hippie back in the 1970s and it's now not something I would suggest people do.

Back then I was, like many others, looking for some way to change things that didn't involve blowing people up or shooting politicians. The world around me looked pretty grim – well, let's be honest, it was pretty grim. This was a period of immense social unrest, with a distinct lack of personal hygiene (though that last point might have just been me).

There were bombs in the streets and pubs of London and Birmingham, there were constant strikes and political unrest, but there was also an enormous movement for positive change that is very easy to look back on with a jaundiced eye.

The popular notion was that the people who were revolting against the old regime were just a bunch of hopeless hippies getting stoned. Well, although that did certainly go on, an enormous number of so-called hippies dedicated their lives to radically changing the way we lived, the way we thought and the way we interacted with each other. The first seeds of the corporate-adopted 'green identity' movement we are all so sick of hearing about now started with that generation. The big petroleum companies who are desperately striving to appear greener than thou these days were more than happy to appear a vile murky brown in those days. They were raking in money and thought people who worried about the environment were total loons. That's if they were even aware there was an environment, which I doubt. They advertised their particular brand of petrol on TV and clearly didn't give a toss about the consequences.

But the hopeless, lazy, stoned hippies I encountered were struggling to reclaim the city with bicycles, were running organic food shops out of the front rooms of squats, were publishing alternative newspapers printed in derelict buildings which told a different story from the mainstream press – stories in those pre-Internet days that had no other outlet. There was also a very strong ethos of anti-consumerism; people 'made do' as a way of life. My entire peer group wore second-hand clothes. I don't remember anyone, particularly women, going shopping for new clothes. It just didn't happen. If you had turned up at my squat in a new set of clothes you would have been criticized for being 'bourgeois'. That was a pretty hefty insult, one I received from time to time from hardcore make-doers who thought I was trying to be flash because I had a cool bike with ten gears.

I'm not trying to paint a rosy, 'oh, my generation have done all this before and we're better' picture here, because my generation now run the corporations, banks, TV companies, government ... Unfortunately, like all the previous generations, it would appear we really messed it up big time.

I am just trying to reset the perpetual anti-liberal balance that's so popular now. I would be the first to admit that most consumer stuff in those days was dire and you wouldn't want to buy it anyway. If you go to the Coventry Transport

Museum and look at the cars built in that period they truly were the most ugly and badly made vehicles this country has ever produced.

The fashion was dreadful too. Just look at old clips of *The Professionals*. When I walked past people who dressed 'fashionably' like Bodie and Doyle in the 1970s I laughed, even then. Believe me, being a hose-and-jerkin-bedecked medievalist was positively cool. Making an anti-fashion statement like that was the height of hipness.

What I have wondered about since was how anyone could market anything to my peer group, who were, by definition, anti-consumer, anti-designer label and pretty much anti anything you care to think about.

The old guard didn't stand a hope selling us anything, so much so that, outside the music industry, they didn't even try. They must have known we truly didn't want it.

In fact it would turn out to be the very people we mixed with who found their way to making a fortune out of my generation. Richard Branson (Virgin Group) and Anita Roddick (Body Shop) in this country, Bill Gates (Microsoft) and Steve Jobs (Apple) in America. They managed to create products and services that we would feel comfortable using, proud of using in fact, just as my father's generation were proud to use Triumph or Rover cars.

My generation also went on to produce Tony Blair. He's only a bit older than me, grew up in the same era, liked the same music, had the same long hair when he was young, went to Oxford University at the same time as I did.

OK, that last comparison is a slight distortion of the truth. I wasn't, strictly speaking, a student at Oxford University, although I did learn a great deal while I was there. I worked in the kitchens of an ancient college, mainly washing up, carrying in the groceries and making toast. But then our lives parted and Tony went on to be a political leader who, for reasons I will never comprehend, backed the most blinkered, reactionary regime the world has ever seen and invaded the wrong country for the wrong reason at the wrong time, while I went on to be a radical performer, sitcom actor, semi-successful novelist and small-time TV presenter.

So his actions have had a little more global impact than mine, but I comfort myself with the fact that I never started a war or fiddled my religion to get my kid out of the state education system. Or even pretended to be a socialist so I could get into power.

My generation, who supported him and rejected the bourgeois attitudes of their forefathers, but joyfully went on to fuel the property boom, the dot-com bubble, the explosion in private education, hedge funds, the ubiquity of long-haul flights, second homes in Tuscany and the constant need for sun-dried tomatoes, are anything but heroes. All those clichés are true, so we have nothing to crow about, but ours is also the generation that brought about the personal computer revolution (I am one year younger than Steve Jobs), the breakthrough in communication thanks to the Internet, the dawning of true understanding about what we are doing to our planet. The long-haired hippies who were building the wind generators and solar panels on display at the Comtek festival of 1974 in Bath are now, as people in their mid-fifties, the ones trying to develop alternative methods of powering transport and to create buildings that don't destroy the world they are built in, suggesting that organically grown food might not only be a better thing to eat but, more importantly, be sustainable in the way we produce it.

What I am saying is that people my age, now steadily becoming bitter and disillusioned – note the popularity of the BBC's *Grumpy Old Men* series – should give themselves a break. I would be the first to admit that a yoga-practising, sandal-wearing New Age organic bore is someone to be avoided at all costs, but in some ways it's like religion. We've let the barking-mad zealots set the tone; as always, it's the slightly more gentle people who don't want to ram their ideology down other people's throats who get shoved to the side.

I was worrying about our reliance on oil back in 1972. That was a long time ago and everyone in authority, the Establishment if you like, would have thought someone with my views was a commie, an anarchist or at best just plain bonkers. But we weren't barking, we were basically right. We knew the human race couldn't go on pummelling the earth forever without some kind of adverse consequence. Now, nearly 40 years later, everyone, even George W. Bush, the president of the United States, has finally accepted that we might, now it's far too late, have to do something.

So it's just possible that a global movement of one year of non-consumerism is a good idea. I am certainly not the only person doing it; in fact since I started all I have heard about is other people who are taking the whole project much further.

Just the other week a near neighbour gave me a cutting from the *Sunday Telegraph*; she suspected correctly that I wouldn't have seen it. It's about a woman called Lila Das

Gupta who didn't buy anything new for a year except, she points out, underwear. Well, I went further than Lila. I just carried on with the underwear I started out with and, at the end of the year, my pants were a little bit worn and not suitable for public display. Not that I display my pants in public, not that often anyway, and I'm being treated for it.

In America, the land that invented the shopping mall, not shopping is becoming an epidemic. There are hundreds of 'compact' groups who are reducing their consumption much further than I even considered. Through Internet forums and social-networking sites they are swapping both things and skills in order to try and reduce their consuming needs.

In New York there's a man called Colin Beavan who has become self-proclaimed 'No Impact Man'. He's really gone the whole hog by taking a vow not to buy anything for a year, anything at all other than food. I'm talking no toilet roll, no nappies for his baby, and he's going further. He has not used anything disposable, not travelled on anything other than public transport or his bicycle, not used any electricity, not used a flushing WC or the aforementioned toilet paper, not bought any food that comes from more than 20 miles away from where he lives.

Now, this would be tough if he lived where I do, in the middle of a rural area. At least I've got a garden to bury my, ahem, waste in. I've got farm shops nearby which sell local produce and I've got a wood-burning stove to keep me warm in winter.

Colin Beavan lives in the middle of Manhattan. He has a baby daughter and he won't even buy her disposable nappies.

He uses those old-fashioned ones with a big safety pin like my mum did, the ones you wash and use again.

Judging from what he's written about his experiences (Google 'No Impact Man' for his very amusing blog), he has a great attitude towards the whole thing. Certainly not po-faced and miserable, he confronts his daily challenges with a light heart.

It's also obvious from what he's written that he didn't make this decision for an economic reason, as in he was so broke he really had to cut back. Although he readily admits he's saving an enormous amount of money by walking everywhere (no gym fees and he's lost a lot of weight) and not using any electricity (that means no TV and no computer), it's fairly clear he's not short of a few bob. ('So how does he write his blog if he doesn't have a computer?' I hear you ask. And the answer is, 'Read it and find out.' I don't know, but I bet he's thought about it and possibly uses a free one at the Central Library on 41st Street. I've been there and the staff are charming.)

Clearly that's not why he's doing it. It's an experiment to see if it is possible to live in an urban environment and have zero negative impact on the planet. From what he reports, it's pretty close to impossible, but his experiment has dramatically reduced the amount his family consumes in a year.

Why is he doing it? Well, he can see the damage he's causing not only to the world, but more importantly to himself and his family by constantly being screen-bound, possession-obsessed and struggling for an ever-increasing income. He's just kicked all those problems to one side and concentrated on living.

Why did I do it? I would like to think for primarily the same reasons, but due to my very different circumstances I've had to face very different challenges. What has been amazing for me is, in my very small way, it's made me concentrate on what I do have. It's made me grateful for that rather than being bitter about what I don't have.

I look at Colin Beavan, 'No Impact Man', with admiration. He's going all the way so we don't have to. I'd be the first to admit he's barking mad, but I'm really glad he's doing it.

'By now, I am beginning to see the plus side of not shopping. I spent the day in London, attending meetings about TV and film projects I was working on. Loads of meetings: two in the morning, then a posh lunch with Ed Bye and a man from the BBC before two more about Internet video systems and new media distribution chains, which involved no money changing hands. None of it makes much sense to me but I enjoyed myself, running round like a headless chicken and utterly ignoring the shops I passed.

I haven't been into a shop that didn't sell food or medicine for nearly three months and it's wonderful. I haven't browsed on-line shopping sites either. I've stopped a whole range of consumer-based activities and it isn't hurting.'

I HAVE no idea when the first big shopping malls were built in this country, but I never went to them. I wouldn't even have known they had opened; it wasn't the sort of thing that impinged on my consciousness. I can imagine there might have been an item about one of them in a newspaper I picked up in a café one morning, left on the seat by the scaffolder who was at my table before me. On page six there would have been a report about Frank Carson the comedian, or someone of that ilk, opening Bluewater or somewhere like that. But I never looked at that page because those sorts of papers depress me so much I can never get past page four or five. Yes, I'm a snob and I have learned to live with it.

The first time I went to a real shopping mall was in Los Angeles in the mid-1980s. I was staying with friends, Lizzie and Mike, in the Hollywood Hills – the wrong end of the Hollywood Hills, I should point out, no film stars in that neighbourhood, but it was a beautiful house, with hummingbirds feeding off flowers on the porch. And this wasn't just any old mall, this was the Beverly Mall.

Lizzie and Mike wanted me to see it because it had only just opened and, as the name suggests, it was in the Beverly Hills district of the city. They were very proud of it and told me I would 'totally dig it'. They were proper 1960s hippies whom I had originally met in Amsterdam – long story, I won't go into it, but they were lovely and very hospitable. So we got into their battered car and cruised down Sunset, took a left on La Brea and parked in the multi-storey car park under this truly massive building.

I have been there since and it's a bit run-down now, but back then it was brand new and a state-of-the-art mega-complex of high-end consumerism.

It was so swish even the floor surface in the car park was shiny and made the car tyres squeal like in the movies. As we were parking Lizzie pointed to an enormous car near us. A woman got out and I studied her closely, thinking she was the phenomenon my hosts were referring to. I now know she was the type of woman you could see only in Los Angeles. She was young and slender but with the weirdest beehive hairdo that makes Amy Winehouse look like a vicar's wife. She wore bright pink leggings and amazing dark glasses studded with gems and styled like a 1950s movie star's. However, I soon discovered it wasn't the woman they were pointing at, it was the bumper sticker on her car. It read simply: 'Born to Shop'.

I shook my head in British befuddlement, which pleased Lizzie and Mike. Then he told me, 'You are gonna dig this place, man. It's right out there.'

We rode the elevators up into the mall and it did indeed take my breath away. The sheer scale of the place – you could get a couple of Boeing 747s in there and still have room for a comfortable family home. The floors were glistening polished marble. There were fountains and huge sculptures, lights, high glass-roofed atriums, full-sized palm trees. And people. Thousands of people walking around in shorts, wearing bright shirts, carrying shopping bags and eating ice creams. They all looked so happy: they had well and truly made it because they lived in America and were shopping in the Beverly Mall.

I happily admit I was enthralled and utterly seduced by it all. It was just so wonderful, and it made socialism and communism and equality between all people of the earth, not to mention environmentalism and awareness of the damage we might be doing to the planet, seem so silly and a waste of valuable shopping time. How could anyone criticize the system that produced this shiny bounty? This wasn't some shoddy cheap discount store with a litter-strewn car park; this was a beautifully made building and all the shops were so clean and new they even smelt nice. There were coffee shops and restaurants, a ten-screen multiplex cinema, glass lifts whishing up and down inside the giant atrium.

These things are so commonplace now they are too dull to describe, but you have to remember that there was nothing like this then in the UK. Or rather I had never seen anything like it. And as for the shops – oh, Lord, the endless supply of wonderful goods, and with the exchange rate it all seemed so cheap to me. At this time I could just about afford to get to the USA and back, so I wasn't exactly awash with spending money. I did my best, though: I bought a pair of trousers, socks and T-shirts, boxers and a really nice holdall which I still own.

My hosts bought so much stuff we had to share carrying the load, and these really weren't wealthy people. They worked in the special effects industry on films like *Robocop* and *Terminator*. They were well paid but not mega-buck movie stars by any stretch.

Their attitude would certainly have been what was the point of going to a temple of consumerism and not buying anything? It would be like going to a mosque and just having a chat with your mates.

I remember that mall as a place of huge excitement and optimism. It was a glorious spectacle of colour and life-changing hope. I observed none of the cultural hooks that might allow me to judge or criticize the people who were shopping there. True, a lot of them were very large by British standards of the day, and I mean very large. This was at the height of Lycra fashion, which meant there was a lot of it on alarming display. It was during our shopping expedition that I came up with a new sales pitch for this particular material much to the amusement of my hosts. As we watched a very hefty mom walk past with her equally hefty offspring, I said, 'Lycra, the cruellest cloth.'

I know I shouldn't have made the joke and I felt guilty, but it really wasn't a flattering material if you were anything over a size eight.

Now, on the very rare occasions that I visit a shopping mall, I don't quite have the same experience. I used to think this was because when the British try to copy the Americans we just don't do it very well: buildings more Iceland than Neimen Marcus, car parks spread like an oil spill over thousands of square yards of bleakness around the ugly central building, the emphasis always on bargains and the opportunity to save ££££s.

On my return to the Beverly Mall some ten years after my first visit, when I was filming *Scrapheap Challenge* in LA, I found that something had changed. I don't know if it was just me, but the place looked battered and low-rent. A lot of the stores were closed, fast-food joints had taken over the multi-ethnic food hall and the many security guards looked like extras in a Schwarzenegger sci-fi movie.

I didn't buy anything on that visit, going instead to another mall up the road with a crowd of ex-pat Brits who were working for RDF, the production company that made *Scrapheap Challenge*. This mall wasn't indoors; it resembled a real street, only you couldn't drive along it. It looked quite like the town square in the movie *Back to the Future*. Everything was spotlessly clean and bright, the shops were amazing, brand-new buildings built in a retro style. It was incredibly busy, amazingly hot in the midday Californian sun, and I bought absolutely nothing. I didn't find this place as utterly soul-destroying as traditional shopping malls; at least you could sit outside on one of the immaculate park benches and watch the movie-star look-alikes wander among the crowds. But it wasn't exactly what you would call a 'real' experience.

At the end of my year of making do I went into a fairly large and spanking new mall called West Quay in Southampton. It was right next to the hotel I was staying in while filming for the Channel 5 series *How Do They Do It?* I knew it must have been fairly new because it was all still very swish, with nice glass doors that softly go thrumph when they close and spotless lifts and criss-crossing escalators and all the standard nonsense that we've come to expect in such places.

It was just before Christmas and a year to the very day from when I had made my decision on the beach in Queensland. We finished filming at about four in the afternoon due to lack of light, not to mention the fact that we were all so frozen by the cold wind we couldn't really talk. So I had time to go on my first shopping trip.

I wasn't looking forward to it and it didn't last long. I did buy some new socks and pants, then I looked at some shirts and tried on a pair of trousers but didn't buy them. I returned to my hotel room with a paltry collection of consumer items.

I couldn't do it, even though everything I'd bought I actually needed. I couldn't justify the expense to myself of buying something 'nice'. Since then I have managed to get a pair of trousers in a sale and my posh walking boots, plus a new electric drill and a box of drill bits and that's about it. I am still holding back for reasons that are not at all clear to me. Every time I think about buying something I stop myself. Could it be that I now understand I can be perfectly happy without it?

'End of the tax year, something I am uniquely bad at sorting out, something I have become much more aware of this year. I think this is because even though I have stopped spending any money on myself, no little indulgences, no treats, no big purchase to fret over, we are going through something of a financial crisis and I can't seem to fathom out why. I am now wondering if I decided to stop buying new things because I knew I would have to anyway. Maybe I could see this coming, but, as a self-employed person for something like 30 years, I have made the biggest mistake in the book. I didn't save anything for tax for the last couple of years and now that error is really coming home to roost. This is no longer about some rich bloke getting a bit depressed about consumerism, this is about some average Joe who can't pay the bills.'

WHEN I was a little boy I loved drawing. I could easily spend all day doing elaborate sketches of war scenes or disasters of colossal proportions. Hundreds of little figures moments away from doom as clouds of chaos were about to engulf them. Yes, I know I need treatment and, if this book sells well, I promise I will start.

To balance this rather macabre output I also did drawings of hundreds of little figures building huge towers or bridges. Obviously a few of these would be crushed by massive beams or fall to their deaths, but there was often some semblance of utopian hope in my pre-teen scribblings.

All these drawings were done on the back of what I now know to be building society rate cards. My father brought them home from work. Basically they were big piles of discarded office stationery advertising the super-low interest rates that his particular society had on offer.

Although it was my father's profession to lend money to people, he never borrowed much himself. I also know that any lending he did do to eager young couples was on very tight terms. It was hard to get a mortgage in the 1960s. You really had to be able to prove that you could pay it back and the amounts he lent, judged by today's standards, seem pitifully small. The price of houses during the first 20 years of my life was a very dull subject. Well, it still is, but no one talked about them at dinner parties, not even my dad, and it was his job. My parents bought the house I grew up in for something like £3,000 in 1956. They sold it in 1970 for £3,500. That's 14 years with a mere £500 increase.

The level of personal debt in those days was also very low. Now, as we are all well aware, it is close to unsustainable. The last time I checked (four minutes ago) the level of personal debt in this country was £1.3 trillion, which works out at £52,000 per household. Of course, by the time you read this it will be a great deal more.

I can honestly say I don't know if it matters that we are all in so much debt. Every financial professional I have ever spoken to is always encouraging me to borrow more, while I am obsessed with not borrowing anything. They have even tried the 'cliff fall' test on me. This is one of those hypothetical situations insurance salesmen love to use. You are falling off a cliff and, as you drop to your untimely death, are you worried about the £2 million you owe the bank? The answer is very clearly no. The financial adviser I was talking to told me I'd be laughing all the way down. Actually, I don't think I would be – I have a very vivid imagination and could see myself stricken with utter terror as I fell to my doom. However, the next question then comes swiftly: before you fell off the cliff, suppose you had been saving furiously for the previous 20 years and you had £2 million in the bank which you hadn't spent. How would you feel during those brief seconds before you splattered like a ripe peach on the rocks below? I didn't really think you'd be that worried about the money; in fact I claim it's the very last thing you'd be thinking about, but maybe that's just me. I'd be screaming and trying to grab at the branch jutting out from the side of the cliff. 'There is no branch,' says the smiling financial adviser as she slides the life insurance form across the table towards me and offers a pen.

I am genuinely impressed by people who seem to be so casual about their debt and I'm intrigued by the fact that the British, who as a rule don't like to discuss money, will happily tell you how much debt they're in. Oh, and we all discuss house prices of course. But debt is a subject that spins me into instant anxiety.

I had a good friend a long time ago who trained as an architect, dropped out of college and became a very successful property developer. He once told me that when he owed the bank £200 they were very rude to him, writing threatening letters which stated they were about to start legal proceedings. When he owed them £8 million they were really nice to him and took him out to lunch. Of course, he'd borrowed the £8 million to develop a huge building in the West End of London, so it wasn't like he'd used it to go on holiday to Greece, but we both found the difference in attitude intriguing. He lived a very high-stress life, worked incredibly hard and tragically died at the age of 42 from a heart attack, leaving two beautiful children and a wonderful wife. I truly doubt he was laughing about the fact that he owed the bank £8 million during his last few seconds of life.

There's an intriguing little side note to this story. And remember this is from someone who is anything but superstitious: I have never seen or believed in ghosts or messages from the other side. However, when this good friend died I was in Australia. It was the middle of the day in the UK and the middle of the night in Australia. I woke from a truly fearful nightmare in which my property developer friend and I were in a swimming pool and he was trying to push me under the water in order to get out of the pool. He was very angry and distressed in the dream and I was trying to reason with him in between choking on inhaled water. I woke in a cold sweat and went outside the beach house we were living in truly shaken up. I don't generally wake from dreams, in fact this is the only time I can ever remember doing so, but it disturbed me so much I wrote the dream down in my notebook in order to remember it and tell him about it on my return to England. I should reveal that the dream also involved a woman with whom we had both been involved many years earlier; not simultaneously – I don't want any threesome allegations at my time of life – but clearly there had been a degree of tension around these liaisons. I put the dream down to some sort of anxiety-based subconscious gubbins I was trying to resolve internally.

Three weeks later (this was well before email), I received a letter from a mutual friend informing me of his untimely death. I felt sick with shock. This was the first of my peer group to die so suddenly and unexpectedly. I checked the date in my notebook and it was the same night I had dreamed about my friend. I was dreaming about him struggling for life at what I crudely calculated was the exact time he died. Now, all spooky oogie-boogie stuff aside, how weird is that?

Anyway, back to debt.

The next really difficult thing to understand is the national debt. What a complete mystery that is. If there is anything in our lives which binds us together as one society, it has to be the national debt. Ours is bad enough, but the US national debt is truly staggering, and it's not a new thing. The first time I was in New York, in the late 1980s, there was a huge electronic sign high up on a building overlooking Times Square. It might still be there and, if it is, I bet they've had to expand it. On the right-hand side was a dollar sign followed by a string of numbers which made an international dialling code look short and easy to remember. As you looked slowly right the numbers started changing, each one getting faster and faster until, by the time you reached the numbers on the far right-hand side, they were just a blur. This was showing the national debt, spiralling out of control. I can't remember how much it was, it must have been many trillions, but I do recall that President Bush Senior was in the White House. Surprisingly, to me anyway, during the Clinton administration this figure was drastically reduced, only to be hoicked right back up again when President Bush Junior took the helm. Unsurprisingly to everyone, this is not a piece of information the Bush administration harps on about.

But that's just politics. What I want to know is where the richest country in the world borrows its money from. If I borrow money from the bank to buy a house, it's all pretty straightforward to understand. My dad explained it to me many years ago. All these people save a bit of money in the bank and while the bank has it all, it lends some to other people and charges them interest. Of course, banks charge slightly higher interest on the money you borrow from them than they pay on the money you save with them, that's how they make a profit. Ever seen a small, tatty-looking, low-rent building with a bank in it? Of course not. They make loads of money, so much so that they can afford to swallow the billions they are losing every year through credit card fraud rather than admit that the system is down the Swannee.

But that's another issue. The other thing banks do is borrow from other banks, and buy debts from other banks, and then they make even more money. Unless they blow it, in which case they lose all your money, but strangely never their own. They know better than to leave it in a bank.

So that's us and banks. What about countries?

Countries borrow from, well, where do they borrow from? Other countries? I know America is borrowing from China, which just doesn't make sense somehow. And it's got to end badly, hasn't it?

I know some countries also borrow from the International Monetary Fund, but where does the IMF get its money from? I assume it's borrowed from yet other countries.

However you look at it, our piffling concerns about credit card debt, mortgages and bank overdrafts are but straws in the wind. All the truly rich people I have met know how to borrow a lot of money, that's their big skill. I am rubbish at it and still live in a stupid fantasy land which makes me want to pay it all back and not owe anyone anything. This might be naïve, but I think I would need long-term counselling to overcome my conditioning.

It is also hard to understand what it must be like for young people, even highly educated young people who have just left college, to get their first job, have a bank account, an income, even on rare occasions job security, but then also have a credit card. I get about five credit cards a week sent to me through the mail. I don't mean actual ones, but offers to apply for them, with monstrous credit limits and loads of numbers with percentage signs after them, and mysterious abbreviations like APR. I never even open the envelopes; I just put them in the massive paper-recycling bin we have in the garage. But banks are busting a gut to get us to use more and more credit cards and some people do so very cleverly. I know a man who has literally hundreds of them. He is constantly opening new accounts, transferring his various debts around, only using the cards while they charge zero interest for the first six months, then paying that debt off with another new card. He is incredibly knowledgeable about it, seems to manage to do his job and live an interesting and varied life while he does so. He once tried to help me sort out my financial affairs by suggesting I apply for some cool new credit card which would let me borrow £10,000 for absolutely nothing for six months. I did get the card, which stayed attached to the covering letter on my desk for about a year before I cut it up and binned it. I just couldn't do it. It's not that I don't have credit cards, in fact I have two, but they are both linked to my bank account and are settled each month so I don't pay any interest. Of course, I have to pay for this privilege, a yearly fee of a little more than £100, so the bank doesn't truly lose out.

My reservation about credit cards is that this complex system is so cruel when it goes wrong. It distorts people's lives and drives them to despair. Credit cards are so easy to use, they allow us to consume more and so maintain the economy. They are totally part of our lives and there is nothing a grey-haired utopian old hippie like me can do about it. However, it is just possible I won't have to. I'm not optimistic about this, but logic suggests there has to be an end point, a moment when the system really does start to buckle under the strain. If so many countries, institutions, corporations, companies and individuals owe so much money to each other which, on a day-to-day level, is never actually paid back and there are finite resources on the planet, surely there will come a point when the financial merry-go-round starts to squeak. Whenever I listen to economists talking on the radio or on podcasts, and I listen to these more than is possibly helpful to either myself or my family, I am fascinated by their take on the world. It is truly very different from mine and I respect their knowledge, obviously mitigated by the fact that some of the more strident economists of the last 50 years have been proved catastrophically wrong.

So how much debt did I have at the start of my year of not buying anything new? Roughly £245,000. See, I can say that, it's not embarrassing, it's just a fact. How much debt did I have at the end of my year of not buying anything new? Roughly £245,000. So, on a purely financial level, the whole effort has made absolutely no difference.

Double Standards

EASTER
2007

'Lovely weekend with the kids, at home, not doing much, not going anywhere, not spending any money. I say lovely, it was lovely for me, I don't think Judy or the kids will hold this period of their lives as some glowing moment of joy. It's a feeling I am more and more aware of, after years of ambition and struggle for more, I now seem to have a burning desire to have less. The quandary is, I cannot impose this on others and I therefore feel trapped on the treadmill I have created for myself.'

DOUBLE standards is the area where my competitive instinct is at its most honed. I strive for more double standards than anyone else on earth and I think I'm doing pretty well. I became uncomfortably aware of my own double standards as the year wore on. There were so many contradictions in my life, I couldn't think about them without crashing into soft despair. I would often stand in the garden, on my own, asking myself, 'Why am I making a big deal out of not shopping for a year when everything else I do is beyond the pale?' I didn't find the answer.

It's another one of my unfounded, unresearched crackpot theories based on nothing other than the oft-mentioned 50-odd years of experience, but I think people with right-wing views have double standards in their private life and people with left-wing views have them in their public life.

I'm obviously using the Left/Right delineations in their broadest, most catch-all sense. I know there are no longer people around with what were once called hard left-wing views, and the only people with hard right-wing views are British fascists, Christian and Muslim Fundamentalists and the odd Australian red-neck truck driver, but hopefully you know what I mean.

In Britain the Conservative Party espouses family values but its MPs shag around like tarts littering the land with illegitimate children who have to fend for themselves. If they haven't done that, they are found dead on their kitchen tables wearing red tights with an orange full of amyl-nitrate stuffed in their mouths, or they get arrested in a gay strip club which they claim they went into by accident when they were drunk, and of course it's important to remember they are always happily married.

OK, the last one I know something about. You probably don't remember the incident because it came at a time when there was a torrent of scandal in the Tory Party. I don't remember the name of the MP, but he was your classic Tory boy. I worked for many years with a wonderful man called Chris Eymard, who sadly passed away much too young. He was gay, very gay and proud to be so. His boyfriend, Michael, was also very gay and a dancer who occasionally worked in a gay strip club in Soho. One of the regular clients was a smartly dressed man of middle age who would come in at the same time each week and watch Michael do his act. I have to say I never saw Michael's act, but I have a well-developed imagination so let's just say it's a fair guess that it would have been healthily explicit. One day during the show this regular well-dressed middle-aged punter put his hand on the knee of another man sitting next to him who turned out to be what was then known as a 'pretty policeman' – a law officer whose job it was to catch furtive homosexual males trying to procure sex in a public place. What a wonderful use of taxpayers' money, hear hear.

The smartly dressed man was arrested. Michael watched the whole thing take place in front of him. It was soon revealed that this man was a leading Conservative MP who was, surprise surprise, 'happily married' and, according to his statement, had got drunk and walked into the gay strip club by accident. He stoutly proclaimed he had never been there before and it was all a terrible, embarrassing mistake.

Now, let me briefly explain. The exterior of this club was anything but discreet. This was in the good old days when Soho really was a red-light district, not a trendy mid-town hangout full of pleasant bars and TV post-production companies. It was dead seedy and the sign outside the club had two words made of neon lights 6 feet high. The two words were 'GAY' and 'NUDE'. It's just one of those stories you remember and I am not going to tell you about the other people Michael the dancer claimed he saw in the front row, but you would know who they were and you might be a little surprised.

Members of the Labour Party, on the other hand, espouse decency and transparency in public life. They are very keen to talk about open government. Honesty, they claim, is everything when you are in power.

They then spend their time trying to fiddle and wriggle their way through swathes of embarrassingly obvious rule-breaking corruption scandals. They accept money from dead dodgy donors and claim they didn't realize they were breaking the rules and laws they themselves created. They also publicly support the state education system while sending their own children to, ahem, specialist schools, or Catholic schools, or specialist Catholic schools. However you try and spin it, they send their own children to private schools, on which more in a moment.

Of course, not wanting to be left out of this mess of human existence, I have endless double standards which have at times ripped me to bits internally.

My lifelong battle with pornography is a good example. I think it's wrong, I think it shouldn't exist, I think it damages the way men and women relate to each other, I think it is exploitative and corrupting. I also love looking at it.

I know you can't ban it, because 1) it's just no longer technically feasible to do so, and 2) if it was illegal it would be even more enticing (and there's plenty of historical evidence to support this particular theory).

Another classic double-standard area is private health

care, something I have always been opposed to. I resent the fact that some of the tax I pay goes towards funding the National Health Service, which is the only institution in this country that trains doctors. Some of these doctors then go and work in the private medical system and I don't blame them. I would if I was a doctor. But the private medical insurance companies are making a mint out of my taxes and yours. They don't have to train their own staff; they get them wonderfully pre-trained for nothing. And it doesn't take much to work out what would happen to the cost of private medical insurance in this country if the insurance companies had to train their own doctors. Obviously it would go through the proverbial and make it impossible for 90 per cent of the people who pay for it now to be able to afford it.

Having said all that, while nurturing my long-held bias against the private medical system, when we are in Australia I don't hesitate to use their private medical facilities. How double-standardy is that? Not to mention that if I was ever put in the position where my wife or children's health was under threat and there was no rapid alternative, I would sell the house and pay for private treatment without hesitation.

Then there is private education. Oh boy, this one is a doozie and has really torn me apart in recent years. I thought I understood the intricacies of double standards until this one hit me. Of course, parenting instantly loads you with a heavy overcoat of double standards, so I shouldn't have been surprised.

For many years I was the proud parent of two children who attended a state primary school within a three-minute walk of where we lived. They literally had to walk over a field to get there; no motorized school run for us, no waiting in traffic jams in a massive four by four with the kids strapped in the back five days a week. We always walked to school.

Then, for reasons which, believe me, are far too dull and complex to go into here, also unfair to the various teachers involved in the whole debacle, we were put in a position where we felt we had to remove our children from this friendly local school and send them to a private one 20 miles away. Out comes the car every morning, then we drive them into the local town, sit in traffic jams and pay through the nose for the privilege.

Within days of them starting there I found the situation close to impossible to live with. My ease at coping with double standards had suddenly found its limit. I have always been vehemently opposed to private education. I think it's divisive and unfair and a very concrete way of guaranteeing the present unbalanced status quo. Not a popular view and very few of my friends, peers, family or anyone I know would agree with me. This is compounded by the fact that a great many of my lifelong friends attended private schools and they are all really nice. That's not the point, however.

In their book *Freakonomics*, authors Steven Levitt and Stephen Dubner report on a massive 20-year-long survey into education following the lives of over two million US children. In it they present evidence that gives the lie to so many common assumptions pushy middle-class parents have about their children's education. In terms of exam results it doesn't matter where you live, it doesn't make any difference if you try to educate your children out of school time by taking them to museums, it doesn't matter how rich or poor you are or what race you are or what school they attend. Some children do well with a range of negative circumstance mitigating against them, while others do poorly with all the advantages they could possibly be offered. However ...

One of the few things that will actually make a difference to a child's prospects of passing exams is if both parents are middle class, university-educated and send their offspring to a private school. If this happens the child will do better.

This was a piece of information I really didn't need. I had next to zero support for my discomfort from my entire child-rearing peer group; they couldn't understand why I was having a problem with it. I could afford to send my children to a really good school, so why didn't I? They were my children. I loved them and wanted them to be happy and successful people when they matured.

Of course, I blame the Labour government. Of 1945. That's when they had the one and only chance to abolish the private education system in Britain.

OK, I know that sounds radical, but just stop for a moment and imagine this country with no private education system, no Eton or Harrow, no Stowe or Bedales, no Cheltenham or Roedean. An education system with no get-out clause for the wealthy and privileged. If they had to send their kids to the local school, how bad would that school be? How run-down would the schools be, how under-staffed by teachers with a low social position, low self-esteem and even lower morale?

It would obviously improve every school in the land overnight. There would be great crowds of pushy harridan mothers hectoring the education officials, hassling the head, pushing and shoving at the school gates for better facilities, more teachers, smaller class sizes, organic locally sourced school meals, extra sporting facilities. But what did the post-war Labour government do? Nothing. Not a state-funded sausage.

An education act had been passed during the wartime government of national unity by Rab Butler which made education compulsory up to the age of 15. This was seen as a good thing and it laid the foundation for the education system I went through in the 1960s and 1970s – the 11-plus, O levels, grammar schools, secondary modern schools, all that gubbins.

Then, in 1945, the post-war Labour government was voted in on a massive landslide. And this was a proper Labour government, not like Tony and his crew. These were good old-fashioned socialists who claimed to be totally committed to reforming education and making the country a fairer place for all citizens.

Of course, they utterly failed to do anything about it. I have always believed this is a result of your classic leftist double standards. These Labour MPs were all sending their children to private schools, of course they were. I'm sure if you researched long and hard enough you could find one or two who didn't, but it's this sacrosanct thing, isn't it: 'It's my child's education and I have to decide what's best, that's my duty as a parent.' I think this is the most wonderful example of British double standards.

When I went to primary school (state) my best friend was a boy whose dad was high up in the local education authority. This man had a very posh accent and they had a bigger house than ours that smelt of posh food. Even their dog smelt posh; ours was well rough.

I can remember being in his car on the morning of a Conservative election victory. This would have been in the 1960s, Ted Heath I imagine, although I didn't pay much attention at the time.

My *Daily Mail*-reading dad was 'chuffed to bits' at this news, while my friend's very posh *Guardian*-reading dad was fuming and predicting the end of civilization and a decent way of life. This man was Old Labour through and through.

I want to remind you that he actually worked for the local education authority, that was his job, his speciality. He ran the schools I attended, he made decisions about the budgets the schools had to spend, the teachers they employed, the curriculum they taught.

After finishing primary school, did his son go to the local grammar school like me? Up the road, not far away, with very high academic standards which would obviously soon be slightly lowered by my attendance but nonetheless a highly successful school.

Did he buggery. My friend was packed off to a private boarding school somewhere in Oxfordshire, along with his brother and sister. More double-standardery!

So now here's me, the man who is making do for a year, not buying anything new, challenging the consumerist hegemony like some Soviet worker in a propaganda poster holding up a rivet gun (maybe video camera) and looking bravely towards the future, and all the while my kids are at private schools that are so expensive the average family simply would not have the option.

Oh yes, when it comes to double standards, I am up there with the most committed lefty Labour politician whose son or daughter doesn't go to school in Hackney, where their constituency is, but attends Bedales in Hampshire because of their special educational abilities, um, or something.

During the summer my wonderful but let us say challenging son made it very clear that he thought his private school was 'gay' and all the teachers were 'sick freaks' and he wanted to go to the local state school, where all the kids he grew up with were going. This caused more than a little stress in our never entirely laid-back family life, but that is what finally occurred.

At the present time my son is at the local state comprehensive, he's very happy and doing very well. My daughter is at the local expensive private school and she's also doing very well and is very happy. The only two people who are not very well or very happy are their parents, but we've just got to get over it.

Obviously the state of affairs in my family is very possibly one of the reasons behind my original decision to stop shopping, although I have to say I wasn't consciously aware of it at the time. However, there is a state of mind that simply can't be achieved without history, a state of mind that no matter how hard I tried when I was young and uncompromising I would not have been able to comprehend. Not just individual history, but the shared history of a family; the battles, discussions and decisions you make over 20 years all build up into a palpable reality.

My decision to stop buying anything was a reaction to this situation, because by definition something as big and complex as a shared family history is uncontrollable by anyone in it and I am a control freak. I'm not proud of that fact and I struggle on a daily basis to relinquish some deep-rooted need to control my world and the people in it.

This might manifest itself in the way I turn off lights when no one is in the room, or pick up socks and damp towels when the children have had their showers and left them lying around. It might be the endless struggle between Judy and me as to who is the housekeeper, because we both do it and, dare I say it, neither one of us is that good at it and we don't even do it in a compatible way.

When I think of myself on that beach in Australia, toiling away with the double standards I live with, the ability to make one individual decision which would affect me but no one else was tantalizing and liberating. It might have started out as a desire to show my family there was a way of living that would be different from the one we had all grown used to. If that was the case, then it's rather tragic, but what it turned into was something quite different, something far more personal and internal which had no real effect on the family at all. It gave me time to stop and reflect on what I was really doing with my life, and sort out the things that I felt were truly bad, the wasteful consumerism, and the things which I should just accept and learn to live with, the fact that both my children were happy in their respective schools.

Double standards seem to be part of life and there isn't much you can do about them without being a Nazi. We are so easily corruptible and all I tried to do was define to myself behaviour which was really corrupting and behaviour which was pretty harmless. Not shopping certainly helped me sort that out a little more.

'I have a lot of pairs of socks and they are all very 1970s, I suppose, meaning they are worn out and not very pleasant. I am reminded more and more of that period as the year wears on. It really does feel like it is wearing on at the moment. I accept socks and their condition is a petty anxiety, it doesn't keep me awake at night, but just by buying five pairs of socks I could so easily solve the problem. I'm not going to. I'm going to see what happens.'

AM I the only person who lies in bed at night when I am trying to get to sleep and imagines colossal world-ending catastrophes? Along the lines of nuclear oblivion, multiple meteor strikes, the world literally splitting in two with all the people you love on the other half, the seas rising 80 feet and flooding 90 per cent of the land mass. Or what about the entire population of sub-Saharan Africa walking into Europe looking for food? An invasion by machines of the future bent on the total eradication of the human race, a global computer meltdown, the whole world catching fire as we hurtle towards the sun?

OK, it is just me then, but from experience and observation over the last 50 years I think there might be a self-destructive gene in our make-up that almost desires these things. I admit that I had a great many more pre-sleep end-of-the-world nightmares when I was younger, presumably to do with all-out nuclear war, which seemed a very real possibility in that era. I would imagine seeing the flash through my closed eyelids and wake up as my room burst into flames just seconds before the impact wave shattered everything to oblivion. Hollywood has made enough movies about it, for pity's sake.

So is that the underlying reason for me to stop buying things for a year, the 'No Impact Man' in New York to stop consuming anything for a year and the Bishop of London to stop flying for a year?

Is it because we all feel that the world around us is so out of control that we turn to any absurd change in behaviour in a tragic attempt to stem the tide of chaos and confusion? It does seem to be about control, yet there is no way we can control our lives, so it's a futile struggle.

Is it also possible that feeling the world is out of control and we have no power to do anything to change it is mildly encouraged by those in power?

Looking back now, with the benefit of hindsight, the notion that the world spent 40-odd years on the brink of nuclear war is comical, absurd or, looked at another way, a simple lie. The Russians were never going to invade the West; they were just as convinced that we were poised ready to invade them. I don't care what flavour of conspiracy theory you subscribe to. I also don't believe the NATO countries were planning an invasion of Soviet Russia at any time during the Cold War. It was all nonsense.

When all-out nuclear war seemed a real possibility, ah, those were simple times, a clear and obvious enemy that was 'over there' as opposed to living among us. That theory lasted a hell of a long time.

But there's a clue: the word 'seemed'. Nuclear war *seemed* a real possibility. In the West we were endlessly told by our governments that it was a very real possibility, the Soviet Union was hell-bent on world domination and we in the West had to defend ourselves by spending a massive chunk of our gross national product on nuclear weapons.

It was a cruel joke that kept the powerful in power and the rest of us in the dark. In just the same way as the Iraqi weapons of mass destruction we were told about clearly never existed, the Soviets had no intention of bombing anyone and were terrified of us, and, when you think about it, rightly so.

I worked in St Petersburg just after the Iron Curtain rusted away and it was very clear that Russia had virtually no military capability except maybe to defend itself had NATO tanks rumbled towards it across the German plains. Of course, the conspiracy-theory master plan was that the West threatened the Russians so much and they, having experienced an invasion during the Second World War, which cost in excess of 20 million lives, were so paranoid that they spent everything they had on weapons, ran out of money, just like the Whitehouse and Whitehall hawks had hoped, and hey presto, they collapsed.

That seems very plausible, except for the following facts. I never met a Russian who didn't speak English and they all read literature, not tabloid newspapers and gossip rags, but proper highbrow literature. This gave the distinct impression that although they might have had bad teeth and fairly unpleasant standards of personal hygiene, under the Soviet regime they must have had an education system that actually worked, so not *all* state funds were being spent on military hardware.

During my time in St Petersburg I once sat on the bumper of a massive ex-army truck in a cemetery just outside the city. I was acting in a BBC drama series called *Grushko* and it was lunchtime. Sitting next to me was an almost cartoon-caricature Russian man – pugnacious-looking battered face, massive forearms and big hands, overweight, in his late fifties, balding and in dire need of a shower. For a while he sat in silence, carefully peeling a beetroot with a slightly worrying-looking knife that could easily have dispatched a couple of Nazis in its history.

Eventually he turned to me and said in pretty good English, 'Who is your favourite writer?'

This was the guy who ran the generator that powered the lights on the set, not the executive producer or the university-educated fixer we had working with us. This bloke was the gaffer. Now, I have no wish to denigrate the wonderful electricians, gaffers and lighting engineers I have worked with in this country, but I have never met one who would sit next to you at lunchtime and ask who your favourite writer was. They might slag off the director or talk about the footy, but in my long experience discussion of contemporary novelists doesn't usually come up.

I was flummoxed and couldn't think of anyone. I read like a swot, I have thousands of books, I write books, I am obsessed with books, and I couldn't think of anyone. I eventually suggested John Irving, the American author who wrote *The World According to Garp* and *The Cider House Rules*.

My corpulent Russian lunch companion continued chewing his beetroot and ruminating. I then felt even more stupid, because it seemed he had learned one sentence in English and my answer was unnecessary. I was wrong. After careful thought he said, 'I too admire Irving's early work, *The Water-method Man* and *The Hotel New Hampshire* and obviously *Garp*, but I feel he has lost his way more recently. Originally he was a very refreshing voice from America, which allowed us to see the nation we feared in a different light.'

I nodded in utter amazement and have never forgotten this man who for so many years previously I had been told to believe was my arch enemy and who wanted to force me to live in totalitarian darkness and terror. He went on to suggest some Russian writers I might enjoy, hoping they had been translated into English. I did make a note of the names and looked for them on my return home. Nothing, no one had heard of them.

Of course, we haven't had the Cold War for a few years; now we just have the endless threat of terrorism, which is the same thing slightly modified to enable the powerful to hold on to power. Whereas in my youth the Left–Right argument was the mainstay of political life, those distinctions have been utterly erased.

For the younger among you, the old view was that the Right was obsessed with guns, the military and individual freedom to make money out of poor people, and the big fear was communism. They pretty much controlled the status quo because they were much better at understanding power and didn't let guilt and shame get in their way.

The Left supposedly struggled for a fairer, more humane world where the difference between the richest and poorest was minimized and the big fear was fascism. All laudable stuff, but, of course, in the process this crushed any individual endeavour and made life miserable for everyone except those in power, who might lose that power if we disagreed with them in any way and the cruel right-wing capitalists would win, which meant that's what we wanted.

Now both Left and Right have learned the efficacy of having a single deadly enemy to fear. Anyone in power will tell us that evil people are trying to kill us and we should therefore give up all our freedoms and allow torture and imprisonment without trial and have our every move monitored by CCTV cameras.

On a slight side issue, we can be proud that as citizens of the UK we are the most monitored on earth. In the last ten years the government has spent over £208 million installing CCTV cameras in our towns and cities. Personally I don't mind, I love cameras and whenever I see one I look into the lens and smile. You never know, maybe the officer in the control room who's watching it might recognize me. 'Look, there's that bloke off YouTube. I think he might be buying something new!'

So, we have been told to be scared of elusive enemies for years, there is absolutely nothing new in that. George Orwell saw it in 1948 when he wrote *Nineteen Eighty-Four*; it's sort of obvious and quite dull.

But here's a contentious question. Is the oft-repeated threat of global warming caused by our consumption of fossil fuels just another way of keeping us obedient and scared? Is the environmental lobby the strong arm of the old Left, merely Stalinist thugs posing as vegetarians dressed up in hand-woven clothes and recycled leather sandals?

I'll go further. Is my secret ploy in not consuming anything new for one year a cover for a communist takeover of the developed world, a bid to drive us back to a pre-industrial age of agrarian oppression?

This is, it seems, how the Jeremy Clarksons of the world would have it. I endlessly come across people who feel they are being unfairly criticized when all they are doing is going on holiday four times a year, buying huge quantities of consumer goods they don't really need or driving tens of thousands of miles every year in very large cars with very large engines.

'Where is the harm in having a bit of fun?' they say. 'I enjoy driving my car and I've worked damn hard for the money. I just want to kick back and burn a bit of rubber. Now all I get is constant moaning from do-gooders who want me to cram myself on to a dirty train when I could be cruising along the motorway in my 2-ton SUV, listening to the Eagles on my iPod.'

Actually, come to think of it, that sounds like quite a lot of fun.

But casual observation tells us that the tide is finally turning. Slowly the power-brokers of the world are realizing that this time, just maybe, the bearded scientists in their weatherproof clothes who've been warning about this for years might possibly be right.

My only gripe is: how could this possibly have taken so long? I can clearly remember the oil crisis of the early 1970s, when the lights kept going out and people queued in their dormant cars for hours outside petrol stations. The trains didn't run properly, people got trapped on the underground system in London when the power failed yet again. It really was a grim time and my mates and I thought it was fantastic. At last, we surmised in our candle-lit squats, the capitalist system is crumbling, the profit motive – forcing people to engage in mind-numbing repetitive work to produce shoddy goods to make a very few people very rich – is no way to run society. I remember walking past miles of static traffic in London with some long-haired comrades performing instant street theatre. We screamed that they were all doomed, there was no more petrol, the era of the car was over. 'Cars are dead! Leave them to rot!' we proclaimed. They would all have to get out and walk.

I can also remember the faces in those cars lit by the dreary evening light. They really did look scared. It must have seemed like the nutters were taking over and the whole post-war 1960s boom was over; it was back to the Dark Ages.

Of course, we now know that this was a very short-lived victory for my non-aligned anarcho-syndicalist pals, who lived in a squat in run-down Islington. For a start, the house where we all squatted, located in a scruffy old square at the back of King's Cross Station, is now worth at least £4 million, because during the following 30 years, admittedly with the odd glitch, we have seen unprecedented economic growth, a staggering increase in the wealth of the general population of this country, and not only that, we now have more cars which use more petrol than we could ever have imagined.

The oil didn't run out; it was merely that the people we were taking it off wanted a bit more money for it. And we gave it to them – boy, did we give it to them. Only now the destabilizing effect of that massive, sudden and utterly unregulated increase in wealth in the Middle East is starting to come back to haunt us.

What has happened in my life is the direct opposite of everything I expected and confidently predicted when I was 18. I was convinced the system I had been born into would rapidly collapse and we would only trade locally, we would all live in non-hierarchical self-supporting communes, black and white, gay and straight, totally at ease with each other.

I think it important to explain that I was strongly influenced by books rather than people at this time. I was always looking for some sort of hero when I was young and I was always let down. It was safer to read books by dead blokes and not know too much about them. William Morris being a good example. I loved his beautiful book *News from Nowhere*, published in 1890. It was written at the height of industrial expansion in this country and saw a possible future totally at odds with the world Morris lived in, and completely unlike the one that has actually come about.

In the book the narrator awakes from a deep sleep to discover himself in the same location but the date is now 2003. As he explores this strange world he discovers it's a kind of socialist Utopia. There is no private property and working is seen as a pleasure not a chore. He journeys along the River Thames, aided by a sturdy, eminently sensible and utterly socialist boatman. Everything made by man is beautiful and carefully crafted – after all, it was William Morris who helped found the Arts and Crafts movement of that period and you can still buy his wallpaper designs in Liberty on Regent Street in London if you have enough money.

There are no cars, planes, trains, factories or anything remotely ugly. There's no Internet or Sony PS3s or Taliban. Everyone has a beautiful small house surrounded by a beautiful garden where they grow wonderful food. There is no money, no banks, there are no prisons and everyone is totally happy.

Reading that book made me want to go there, it made me want to help create a society like that, and I suppose in some ways I did try to do it. I learned how to make shoes by hand, I lived in shared communities, I became a 20th-century middle-class gypsy living in the back of a truck for two years, but eventually the juggernaut of reality and political expediency shoved me along without hesitation.

There wasn't a nuclear holocaust, the politicians of the age seemed to sort out some sort of peace accord, the oil didn't run out, the economy didn't collapse, the miners didn't win their strike, heavy industry did move from our shores to be replaced by service industries, computers stopped being a weapon of the powerful and became a tool of the many. I want to point out again that I have never been someone who harks back to a mythical golden age when things were better. I truly think, for most people, things are much better now.

I'm glad I was a punk rocker with flowers in my hair. In '77 and '68 revolution was in the air, but only in a very small minority of cases. Most people just went to work and paid their mortgage, got their kids through school, grew old and died.

I have also learned that if, say, you were a journalist and your job was presenting the news, which story would you rather tell: 'Generally everything is OK, not much has happened, most people are more or less happy, it looks like things will get a bit better, there are no terrorists around and we don't need to go to war anywhere,' or 'The economic forecast is pure doom, your house is worth nothing and interest rates are about to sky-rocket, you are grossly obese and your neighbour is a terrorist with chemical weapons, which is why most people are really depressed, and they're right to be, because everything is about to get much, much worse'?

I think it's worth reminding ourselves that 90 per cent of doom prediction is pure spin, but that other 10 per cent is really scary.

These anxieties have all come back to me this year and I think they did as a direct result of not buying anything. If you can stand in a shop and try something on, buy a new shirt, blouse, trousers, skirt, shoes or handbag, it takes time and energy and you can use this activity to stop yourself worrying about the things you feel you cannot change. When people are shopping they are not that concerned about terrorism or nuclear war, pollution or CO_2 emissions, they are worried about that new coat and whether it will go with those boots they've just bought. I have spent the last 20 years living the normal life of the era, worrying about money, the children, my relationship with my wife, the house, the car, my career, the electricity bill. I haven't thought what it all means because I haven't had time. My friends are all doing the same. I have lost touch with the gentle beautiful people who don't engage in this monstrous and unwinnable race of rats. They live on the west coast of Ireland, or up in the Hebrides, in isolated Italian farmhouses or the Mojave Desert, anywhere a long way away from the chaotic centres of commerce, capitalism, the media and consumerism, and I never see them. I know I should make the effort but I never do, I just get the occasional email or Christmas card from them saying they are still around, poor, peaceful and happy. They are, almost without doubt, anxious as well, maybe for different reasons, but they still experience it. I have come to accept that it is part of the human condition, and in a way it shows the true joy of being alive.

I decided during my non-consuming deliberations to embrace my anxieties and relish them. They show me that the rest of the time life is worth living; all anxiety is doing is pointing me to the good things I might lose if I die. Surely that's a good thing?

Bloody hope so.

Silence

MAY
12
2007

'It's Buddha's birthday apparently, not that I know much about him. I am beginning to enjoy the new state of mind I find myself in. I now have periods of time when I truly don't want anything. The only discomfort I have is that I want to get rid of so much that I do have. This is quite the opposite of what I expected and does indeed take me back to the revolutionary attitudes toward consumerism, wealth creation and job hunting that I was so aware of in the seventies. On the other hand, I'd love a new pair of shoes.'

BECAUSE I am essentially a bit of a thick bloke who's quite good at talking, it took me most of the year to work out the probable reason why a lot of my thoughts during my no-shopping period jumped back a few decades to my formative years. For a while I became annoyed at myself for constantly harking back to the bad old days of the 1970s, but I'm trying to forgive myself now.

Like we all tend to be during our late teens and early twenties, I was a giant sponge. I was busy soaking up ideas and opinions from anywhere I could because I felt like an empty nothingness; nothing had ever happened to me, I had no history.

Now, of course, I have personal history coming out of my ears, history weighing me down like a rock-filled rucksack, and so taking in new ideas becomes increasingly hard.

This is why, I suppose, I started to rediscover some of the old ideas that caught my attention some 30 years ago. I came into contact with all manner of people, from the most kind and benign to the criminally insane, and they all had something to impart. One group of people I met in Oxford during this time casually introduced me to a figure called Jiddu Krishnamurti.

Now, before you jump to conclusions that I joined in with a bunch of pseudo-religious saddos wearing orange clothes, burning joss sticks and sitting in funny positions saying 'Om,' it's important to explain to people who have never heard of this Krishnamurti bloke that he was the absolute antithesis of a guru.

There are so many weird connections in life that make no sense at the time, and only a little more sense many years later as you join up the dots. I can remember as a teenage schoolboy travelling up to London with my first girlfriend, Liz, an Australian who made me read *The Female Eunuch* when I was still a terrified virgin. Bit of a challenge to say the least. She really wanted to go to this little shop near the British

Museum and get a book about William Blake, the poet and spiritualist. I wanted to go to Portobello Road and buy loon pants and joss sticks.

She won. With *The Female Eunuch* in my hippie shoulder bag we went to the small bookshop that was run by the Theosophical Society. I had never heard of this group before, or since for that matter, until I read a little about Krishnamurti the other day.

It was a member of the Theosophical Society, Charles Leadbeater, who watched a little boy playing on a private beach in India in about 1909 and decided he saw some wonderful spiritual power within him. Leadbeater decided that the boy would not only become a great spiritual leader but was in effect the Second Coming. He was groomed by the Theosophists to lead the world from depravity and the spiritual wilderness into a new golden age of enlightenment. If you take a casual look around world history over the last hundred years, it's fairly easy to see he didn't have much of an impact.

The Theosophical Society were a pretty odd bunch to say the least, although they clearly laid the foundations for the influx of Eastern religious practices into Europe and the USA – Buddhism, yoga, meditation, all that gubbins, which is what my very clever girlfriend Liz obviously knew all about.

Anyway, this little Indian kid Krishnamurti was groomed by these people to effectively be 'the one'. They brought him from India to London, where he learned English and pretty much flunked at everything else.

He then went to Australia and stayed in Balmoral, which is where my family and I lived in 2001, and eventually spent some time in the Ojai Mountains in California, where, weirdly again, we recorded an episode of *Scrapheap* in 2002. I had no idea of these connections at the time, so I was quite intrigued when I came across this information. On reflection these are very minor coincidences and I'm certainly not trying to say I have travelled the world in his footsteps, or even followed his teachings, because they haven't so much as crossed my mind in 30 years.

Anyway, when he reached his late twenties he attended a huge meeting in Holland organized by the Theosophical Society where he was confronted with a sea of eager followers waiting with baited breath to finally hear the words of wisdom from the chosen one.

Then, and this is the bit I thought was cool, he told them in a very gentle Indian type of way that it was all nonsense. He explained quietly that he wasn't a guru and all gurus were false. He told them there is no God and there is no one to follow. Truth is a land without paths, there is no 'way' and all ideology is nonsense. Here's a little quote from his speech:

This is no magnificent deed, because I do not want followers, and I mean this. The moment you follow someone you cease to follow Truth. I am not concerned whether you pay attention to what I say or not. I want to do a certain thing in the world and I am going to do it with unwavering concentration. I am concerning myself with only one essential thing: to set man free. I desire to free him from all cages, from all fears, and not to found religions, new sects, nor to establish new theories and new philosophies.

He didn't shout and rant and threaten death to anyone who didn't believe him, he just told the listening crowd not to be fearful. Must have been a bit depressing if you were a disciple who'd been waiting years to find a way to avoid the pain of life and the fear of death ...

Of course, what I take from his words is if you can find the ability to experience the void of existence without fear, then you don't need to do anything to fill that void. Like shopping.

Sometimes, when I remember, which isn't often, I like to sit in my garden and, instead of imagining global disasters, allow myself to be silent. To experience the void of silence, the fact that there is nothing, no heaven or hell, no afterlife, no spiritual supreme being keeping a watchful eye on me. There is nothing, a void, an immense and endless hollowness.

If you can do this, and I find it really hard, not to mention quite frightening, it does provide great relief to the soul, relief from the struggle and pain of living and trying to understand how things work, how people work, how society or religion works. All those are important and I relish them, but when I remember to relish the void, the emptiness that is truly at our centre, I find it very comforting.

Not buying anything brought this back with a force I truly didn't expect, because, thanks to my relative wealth and material comfort, I had been filling my inner void with desire for things, things like personal achievement, fame, adulation, success. Things I could own or control that I believed would enhance my life filled my every waking moment. Well, that's not 100 per cent accurate: even at the epicentre of desire, in the chaos of debt management and spending lust, I suppose I knew it didn't really do anything to make me happy or mean anything on the spiritual front.

Consuming doesn't help us to be happy or peaceful any more than politics or religion does. Acceptance of the void, on the other hand, has been a great step towards inner freedom for me.

Just to add a piquant note of reality to this blissful discourse, the other evening I got back home after a fairly intense round of meetings and filming days, voice-overs and logistical planning in London. I stopped the car at the end of my long trip and sat for a moment reminding myself of the importance of finding time to just be still under the stars and gently attempt to allow the silence to engulf one. I got out of the car and was about to turn and get my bags from the back when I screamed in alarm. My delightful, imaginative and occasionally challenging son had crept up beside the car while I was ruminating, crouched down beneath my field of vision, only to shout out like a demented demon as I stood up. My daughter was hiding behind the garage wall and clearly found this spectacle highly amusing. Louis was full of hysterical laughter and the ecstasy of victory: 'That was soooo funny, Dad. Looked like you crapped yourself.' Lovely child.

I was drawn back immediately into the maelstrom of our chaotic family life – endless lists of drop-off and pick-up times, household chores, general repair and maintenance duties – and it was only when I went to bed that night that I remembered my promise to myself to reflect on the void. Needless to say, I didn't go and stand out in the garden in my jim-jams, I just fell exhausted into bed.

Just in case you are interested, if you've never come across him before, you can listen to Krishnamurti through iTunes or YouTube and make up your own mind. I say that with some hesitation, because it sounds like I'm a follower and, as he tirelessly explained, if you become a follower you really are missing the point.

'Finally got my watch back from the repairers, and no surprise really, it cost more than buying a new watch. I suppose I should have just made do without a watch for a year. I can see the time on my mobile phone, I don't need a watch and I now regret taking it in to be repaired. It gets more complicated as the year wears on. I mean, the bits inside the watch are probably new. Damn.'

IF I'm honest this is really where stopping shopping started for me, and the extraordinary power this one simple system has unleashed must be acknowledged.

A few years ago two young men, Chad Hurley and Steve Chen, wanted a system with which they could share their home video clips in the same way that many websites like Flickr allow users to share photographs. The premise was that straightforward. It was a totally Californian idea, very Web 2.0, all about community and sharing and, of course, quite staggering amounts of money.

They unleashed this simple-to-use application in early 2006 and when I first stumbled across it, in May 2006, it already had over a million or so regular users. Within a few months it was delivering over a hundred million videos a day, and this number is steadily climbing.

Amazing as this might seem, when you compare it to the amount of people who watch old-school TV each day, which casual research tells me is around the 3.5-billion mark, it puts things into some sort of perspective.

That said, you can't put your own programmes on the telly with three clicks of a mouse – even if you work in the TV industry for a living, it's still incredibly hard. Believe me, I try all the time.

Putting your programme on YouTube is incredibly simple if you've got all the bits and bobs you need. I admit I'm lucky, I already had them in abundance, so it was a very small step for me.

My golden rule with offerings for YouTube is that I cannot spend longer than one hour making them. That includes having the idea, setting up the camera and lights, recording the show, editing it on my computer and loading it up on YouTube.

I suppose the only way I cheat is while it is loading I start doing something else, so I don't factor that part into my one-hour production time.

As soon as it goes public there's an audience out there, especially if you have a few people who've seen your stuff before. YouTube alerts them that there is a new video of mine ready to see. At the time of writing I have had just short of 300,000 people watch my made-in-an-hour efforts, and every time I put something new up I seem to gather a whole new bunch of people.

This was all just good fun until I made my decision to stop shopping. I called it 'making do', which soon became an irregular series of updates on my own channel. (On YouTube, search for 'making do' and you'll find it.)

The first of these 'vidcasts' I recorded as I was walking along the beach in Australia, the day after my fateful shopping trip to the mega mall. The response to that was so unexpected it made me realize something: that I have the senses of an old showman. I've been working as a performer and writer for 30 years and as soon as I get a reaction from an audience, I take it on board. I thought to myself, 'Hey, they like this one, I'll do some more.'

In many ways that's what kept me going for the year. I started to build up an audience for the idea and I didn't want to let them down. If I was a true artist I wouldn't have reacted like that. I would have ignored the audience and continued to follow the direction my artistic impulses led me. But I'm not. I've spent years standing in front of audiences trying to make them laugh, with varying degrees of success, so when I got a reaction, that was it.

In any case, stopping something like that halfway through would have been like a comedian standing in front of an audience saying, 'During the war, my dad said to me, "You don't need to worry about the bomb unless it has your name on it." That was fine for me and my dad. Thank you very much and goodnight,' and then walking off. (That's an early Paul Merton joke, by the way, and the punchline is, 'But our neighbours, Mr and Mrs Doodlebug, weren't so happy about it.')

So I had to stick with it until the bitter end, when everything was going wrong and running out and all I wanted to do was buy something new.

A very good example of how this casual observation affected me was when I stopped at a garage near Shrewsbury in August 2007. I was returning from a dusty day's filming in North Wales and needed to buy petrol. Clearly, had I been following the far more fundamentalist approach of the No Impact Man I wouldn't have bought the petrol: it was something new and it was for me. This particular garage had a drive-through car wash and, as I could barely see out of the back of my car, I paid for a car wash, drove home and thought nothing more of it.

About three days later I noticed there was a small discussion taking place on my YouTube message board. The young man who served me in the garage was apparently a regular viewer of my videos and had questioned if a car wash didn't in fact count as something new.

I eventually made another video to respond to this, claiming that a car wash was a service and not a new product. Pretty weak, I admit, rather like a government minister on the *Today* programme trying to worm his way out of an obvious blunder. My watchful YouTube audience then discussed this further and it was generally accepted that a car wash was within the bounds of what I had set out to do. I was involved in the community, just as Chad and Steve had predicted. You don't get feedback like that on TV.

So YouTube is ground-breaking and revolutionary and record-breaking, although obviously not all for the good. I have seen stupid, cruel things on YouTube and I have read vile and loathsome comments that people post more or less anonymously, but it's vital to remember that it has liberated a generation from the one-way street of traditional media. It's knocked the TV industry for six, it's pulled the rug from under us, it has sent us into a flat spin. It's worthy of every cliché in the book.

All I know is, without it, I wouldn't have done what I've done; it's been a two-way street for me. I am a show-off and YouTube gave me a channel to show off on. However, by showing off I suppose I shamed myself into following through. I can honestly say that when I first saw YouTube, I had no idea it would help me get through my year without shopping. In fact even now it makes no sense at all.

'This is not a good sign. I spent an hour today reading speculation about the iPhone, the new mobile gizmo from Apple Computers. I don't want one, I've got a mobile phone, but the fact is I'm still interested in them. I have actively searched the web for information about them, the release date has been anticipated with almost religious fervour by the geek community in the USA. Even at my most consumer obsessed, I don't think I could have mustered that kind of enthusiasm for a bit of electronic trickery, but I admit, I did check the specs.'

BEFORE I stopped shopping I would have described myself as someone who was generally immune to product hype, flashy advertising and the brasher side of the consumer market. Given time to really think about it, there is one particularly glaring exception to this state of mind I have had to face. There is a brand which has been part of my life for 20 years and I am very aware of its developments, new products, swish advertising and clever indirect marketing.

It was in 1987 that I first saw an Apple Mac computer. I was visiting friends in Los Angeles and noticed one in a shop window as we drove by in their battered Volvo. The following day I borrowed a pushbike, not a sensible mode of transport in a city so dominated by the car, and I managed to track down the location. This wonderful machine was in a small store off Sunset Boulevard called the Writers' Computer Store. In the window was a beige computer with an unusual screen. Instead of being in landscape mode, as in being wider than it was high, as we are now used to, the monitor screen was like a sheet of A4 paper. Which is precisely what attracted me to it. At that time I was writing very happily on an Amstrad PCW (Personal Computer Word Processor), the first truly mass-market computer to be sold in England. I'd had it a year and it was revolutionary. Up to that point I had either written by hand or typed on a manual typewriter. Both methods led to copious problems, whether just plain illegible handwriting or typos. The word processor was a revelation. If I made a mistake I could correct it without the use of Tipp-Ex or crossing it out and making a mess. I feel I should explain to younger readers what Tipp-Ex is (or liquid paper, as they called it in America): it's a kind of fast-drying paint that you could brush over your mistake and then type over it. Of course, it stuck out like a sore thumb; you could spot Tipp-Ex a mile off. Let me tell you, the Tipp-Ex method of word-processing was really rubbish.

Anyway, I had already moved on from these old methods of production to the white-hot electronic computer age, even if my computer was, by today's standards, virtually a wind-up gramophone. It had a black screen with bright green letters made up of highly visible, individual eye-burning dots. It did your eyes in after a couple of hours to such an extent that when you stopped work and looked at something else, it would appear to have a red glow around it like an aura. I thought it was cool, but now I wear glasses and I'm slightly regretting that particular side effect.

So, looking at this new computer in the small and very exclusive Writers' Computer Store in Los Angeles was a revelation. It was a moment; it was almost an experience of the divine. This computer had a screen that showed the page you would be writing on as white, with very fine black type on it made of dots so small you couldn't count them individually like you could on my old computer. The effect on the screen was that it really looked like paper, it was easy to read and the screen showed a full page at a time. I went inside and asked the rather stern and forbidding assistant about it. I told him I was a writer from England and I had never seen anything like this before. I didn't even ask him how much it was – I didn't need to. He told me with pride, in a way that could only be construed as him being able to tell at a glance that I couldn't afford it. The price, he explained slowly, for this particular model, was over $5,000. He added the term 'fully configured', which meant nothing to me. I smiled and nodded, saying I would be back the following week to pick up the fully configured thing, then left the shop and got back on my bike.

Two years and a lot more red auras later, I was covered in rubber, working on the BBC sci-fi sitcom *Red Dwarf*, when one day during a rehearsal Rob Grant and Doug Naylor, the genius writers behind the show, informed me that they wrote the scripts on an Apple Mac, just like the one I had seen in Los Angeles.

It is important to point out that at this time, the late 1980s, computers were only just emerging from the laboratories of universities and the underground bunkers of paranoid superpowers. You didn't see them in shops; you had to hunt them down to obscure warehouses on the outside of town. They were esoteric mysteries. There was no PC World; there was no one you could ask about them because no one knew anything. Or not in my world. Obviously there were people who knew all about them, one being Steve Jobs, another being Bill Gates. They knew an alarming amount about them and were already rich beyond anyone's dreams.

I made Steve Jobs just a little bit richer when, at the end of recording a series of *Red Dwarf*, I bought my first Apple Mac computer. For those of you interested in such techie data it was an SE 2/20. It had a minute 8-inch black-and-white screen, a keyboard and mouse, and a printer that was so heavy you had to get a friend around to help move it.

It cost so much money I don't even want to write it down, it's too painful a memory. It was slow and could only run one program at once, but then I could only afford one program. I loved it and wrote three novels and one screenplay on it the first year I had it. I still have it and, although I haven't tried using it for many years, I think it still works. It never crashed or froze; it never needed updating or software patches. It stored your work, printed it out and that was it. No Internet, no email, no movie editing, nothing like that.

Because I travelled a lot I wanted to be able to take this wonderful tool with me. On my first visit to Australia I carried my Apple Mac SE 2/20 on board in an enormous carrier bag. It was incredibly heavy and unwieldy; I had to get special permission to take it with me. I cannot believe I did it now, but we were planning on being in Australia for four months and I had a lot of work to do. It was a pain but I got it there, set it up in a house next to the beach and reached a state of divine creative grace. To be somewhere that beautiful and still be able to write – it was bliss. I did the work but then, of course, I had to haul the damn thing all the way back home.

In one way you could say that because I bought a product that did what it said on the box, I experienced deep consumer satisfaction. So much so that when the company introduced a new version which was portable, a laptop, as soon as I had the money I bought one.

Now, 20 years later, I do not know how many of these wretched machines I have bought, truly I don't – it's too many to recall. I know that at present we have no fewer than nine fully functioning computers in our house, I have given away four or five and I have had to recycle that many again when they finally gave up the ghost. It's shocking really, but there is no point denying they have changed my life.

The machine I am writing this on is a called an iMac. It has a processor about 6,000 times faster than that of my first machine, with a storage capacity that is 12,500 times greater, memory that is 10,000 times greater and a screen about six times as big, with millions of colours, which uses less electricity and fewer harmful chemicals. It is connected to the Internet, can edit video to a greater extent than the first editing machine I used (which cost over £100,000), can record 600 tracks of audio, can take pictures, make free international phone calls and burn or play DVDs. It's actually a bit dated and there are far faster and bigger versions already available, but I'm not buying them for the very simple reason I don't need to.

What this tells me, though, is that the journey from teenage medievalist to techno junkie has been long and not without mishap.

The very first sitcom I was ever in was written on a computer. It was called *The Corner House* and was broadcast on Channel 4 in the mid-1980s. I regularly pray that Channel 4 never feels the need to repeat it. Yes, it was that good.

I also co-produced and co-wrote this sitcom, and on one particularly memorable night my co-writer, Chris Eymard, and Seamus Cassidy, then an assistant commissioning editor at Channel 4, chain-smoked and rewrote the entire six half-hour episodes of the series.

It was great. We really tightened the structure, built up the characters and back story. We laughed and congratulated ourselves on our wit and brevity. The room was a mess, paper everywhere, overflowing ashtrays and coffee cups, half-eaten doughnuts and the Amstrad, green letters on a black screen, and everything we looked at had a red glow.

At about five-thirty in the morning we decided we had finally finished. I had done all the typing as the other two paced around and chained it. I had been sitting motionless for 12 hours solid. I pushed back my chair to stretch my crippled legs, not realizing that the power cable to the computer had somehow become twisted around one of the legs of the chair. Fzzt.

The computer died. Power off, nothing. The dive from exalted achievement to utter despair was vomit-inducing. We hadn't saved a thing. You couldn't, really. Saving stuff required you to endlessly swap ultra-low-capacity floppy disks, which was what I had intended to do after we had a celebratory cup of coffee and another fag.

We never got back to the level we believed we had achieved on those scripts, and if any of you are unlucky enough to have seen any episodes of this less-than-memorable part of Channel 4's illustrious history, you may well nod in agreement.

I can honestly say that Mac computers seem more reliable than others, although I did have a Mac laptop once that only typed the letter B, and it did it for days. I tried to stop it, but as soon as you opened a document it just filled thousands of pages with endless bbbbbbbbbbbbbbbs.

I've had horrendous hard-disk failure, software glitches, kernel panics – I have no idea what they are but they sound good – motherboard burnouts, battery-overheating issues, but I am now a long-time back-up junkie. There are presently about 14 copies of this manuscript, some on my own array of hard drives, some on a USB keyfob I keep with me at all times, some on a server farm outside Reading, some on another server farm at Cupertino in America, some on another server farm in Tennessee, and more on a DVD I keep in my safe.

This obsession obviously takes up an enormous amount of time and I would estimate that in the last 20 years I have spent as much time maintaining my computers as I have using them creatively.

So that was another thing my year of making do relieved me of: I didn't buy any new gizmos and subsequently didn't need to spend any time adjusting my systems to deal with them. A valuable lesson for me there, a lesson I promptly ignored, as I did buy several new gizmos and bits of software at the start of the new year, each one of which ate into my time in a way I had completely forgotten was possible.

I think, to sum up the whole 'Mac' experience, I cannot go back to writing by hand, I cannot do without the power the computer gives me to create video, to communicate in a way that was previously impossible. I cannot go back because this little machine has liberated me in a way I could not have dreamed of when I was young. We are stuck with them and they are clearly going to become a larger part of our lives. They are going to get faster and smaller and invade our experience in more and more ways. I am optimistic on the whole, but we do need to discipline ourselves to spend time with real people in meatspace – there is nothing better than a real conversation with real people. Talking to someone in a chat room or via a videophone connection isn't the same, never will be, even if they are in the form of a 3D hologram standing in front of you.

That there is a huge community of Mac fans in the world never ceases to amaze me, even though ostensibly I am one of them. My very old friend Charlie Dancey attended the big annual Mac fest in San Francisco during my year of not shopping (this was when the iPhone was announced). He sent me a picture of a woman staring up at this little gizmo resting in its glass sepulchre. Her face was reminiscent of a cherub staring at the baby Jesus in some 15th-century painting in the Vatican. It was a phone, for crying out loud, not the answer to all human pain and suffering. Much as I would like to believe that a complex piece of machinery can change the quality of our lives, I know this to be false and a path which can only lead to sorrow. I struggle to keep my Mac obsession in check. As I am being reminded now, it doesn't actually write the book for you.

Priusness

JULY
4
2007

'I have been wondering what it would be like to go
the whole hog: to not only stop buying consumer
items like clothes and electronics, books, magazines
and newspapers, but to also stop using any form of
fossil fuel, to not have a haircut or a shave for a
year, to walk or cycle everywhere, to only bathe
in cold water and to bury your poo in the ground
instead of flushing it. I could suggest I do this next
year to my long-suffering wife and children, but I
think I would find myself living alone in a shed in the
woods after a couple of months. I'd have to walk
15 miles every afternoon to get my daughter from
school. It's not going to happen, at least, not by
choice. It may actually happen by necessity and I'm
not looking forward to it.'

PRIUSNESS is another new and little-studied state of the consumer mind. In the late 1990s some very clever engineers employed by the Toyota car giant came up with a system of building a super-ultra-low-emission vehicle, or a SULEV. Not just super or ultra, but super-ultra.

The heightened state of mind known as Priusness can be achieved only when driving the Toyota Prius hybrid car. To call it a mere car is to do it a disservice. The reason for the overlong SULEV title is that, as it moves, this remarkable invention emits the lowest amount of CO_2 per mile of any petrol-powered vehicle on the road at the time of writing.

For the few of you who are not familiar with this increasingly common sight in our urban landscape, the Prius is a petrol-electric car, commonly referred to as a hybrid. It has a petrol engine that powers an electric motor, which is what actually makes the vehicle move.

One thing I never previously understood about trains is that they are all hybrids and have been ever since the demise of steam. In one of those massive throbbing trains you are partly deafened by as they shoot past you on the platform is a massive diesel engine. It is not connected to the drive wheels but is spinning an electric generator which creates the power that is fed to massive electric motors and makes the train move. That's why trains can move off so smoothly – electric motors are good at being as powerful at near zero revolutions as they are flat out.

That's essentially all the Prius has under the bonnet, but this system is backed up by a large pack of batteries under the rear passenger seat, further reducing the need to burn fossil fuel. As you drive along, the petrol engine only starts when the batteries are too low to run the engine, or you, the driver, are calling for more power than the batteries can supply. As you slow down or run downhill, the electric motor turns into a generator and recharges the battery. This means that, particularly in your classic stop–start urban landscape, which is motoring-journalist speak for a traffic jam because there are simply too many cars on the road, the petrol engine is running much less than in a regular car and is therefore releasing far fewer pollutants.

This is why there's no congestion charge for the Prius in central London, why road tax for the Prius is only £10 a year and the insurance rates are very low, and also why there have been instances of aggressive behaviour towards smug Prius drivers recorded around the world.

It has only occurred to me recently that the Prius has a fairly low chance of being stolen. For a start, what cool joyrider would want to be seen in such a naff motor? That's a pretty big deterrent. Then, without the key, this car is impossible to start unless you have a degree in advanced micro-electronics or computer programming, plus three hours to spend dabbling with the on-board computers. Even if a thief managed to get the key, they would probably spend about ten minutes trying to get the damn thing to move. The first time I drove one on my own I sat in the market square in Chipping Norton trying to remember how to do it. I was extra nervous because this is the home town of the oft-mentioned Jeremy Clarkson and I didn't want him to see me sitting in a static Prius, pressing every button and pedal I could find.

The vehicle is computer-controlled; it's drive by wire. The only part with a direct mechanical connection between driver and machine is the steering wheel; everything else has to go through some sort of computer committee. This can be particularly galling if you want to overtake; the Prius is a very bad car to use for high-risk overtaking. You're moving along a country road at 20 miles an hour, following a tractor and peering ahead to see if anyone's coming. The road looks clear and you floor it. Nothing happens. The car continues along silently as it has been for the last five frustrating minutes. Then, once the car's software has been through the many thousands of possible options, once the on-board committee is quorate and in agreement, the petrol engine starts without a shudder and the power starts to kick in, a good 15 seconds after you made the decision that it was safe to overtake. So suddenly you are pulling alongside the tractor as a 30-ton truck comes pelting directly at you.

Now, this isn't because it's a very slow car. I should point out here that electric motors are very powerful. The land speed record for a Toyota Prius, on electric power alone, is 145 miles an hour. So in theory it is perfectly possible to overtake a tractor, but you really need to leave plenty of time for the car to agree with you.

In an urban environment, if you are waiting in traffic and you are in neutral (the car has only three settings: neutral, forward and reverse) and put your foot hard down on the accelerator to rev the engine in frustration, absolutely nothing happens. This is because the petrol engine won't be running; you will be sitting in complete silence. Meanwhile, the Porsche Cayenne, the Range Rover and the Bentley GT which are around you in the same queue (this queue is in a rather smart shopping street in west London, by the way) are using more petrol as they sit unmoving, with their engines merely ticking over, than you would use on a 70-mile journey.

This experience can lead to a deep state of Priusness. Which is not to be confused with cyclism, a holier-than-thou feeling of inner satisfaction which I used to find myself in regularly as I wove expertly through London's stationary traffic on my bicycle.

But Priusness isn't an entirely benign feeling. There are plenty of drawbacks. For a start, the Prius is not a handsome car, in addition to which the visibility is pretty poor and the performance – well, even using the word 'performance' to describe how it moves is a bit silly. It moves, it moves very quietly and it doesn't use much petrol, that will have to do.

Plenty of motoring journalists (of whom more later) have questioned its economy, but let me just state here, I have achieved 72.3 miles to the gallon in my Prius on a 114-mile journey. True, I drove like a vicar from the 1830s who believed if a human travelled at over 45 miles an hour the soul would flee the body, but I got to my destination relaxed and on time. I used 1.25 gallons of fuel to do that journey. On the same journey in my previous car (VW Golf R32), when I averaged 18 miles to the gallon, I would have used 6.33 gallons, and if I had been driving my *bête noire* car, the fabulous four-wheel-drive, 2.5-ton Porsche Cayenne, I would have managed just about 10 miles to the gallon (I'm being kind, it's probably nearer 8 in real life) and used 11 gallons! At current fuel prices that's well over £50 to drive just over 100 miles, and the Porsche Cayenne is as common as muck round where I live.

Now what, I hear you ask, has any of this got to do with

making do? Well, I believe my journey from confirmed petrol-head to hybrid bore was very much part, if not at the root, of the decision I made on the Gold Coast just before Christmas. Basically there was something wrong with the way I was living and I really wanted to change, but I was trapped by circumstance and the well-being of others, which made radical alterations to my life untenable. I was faced with having to practise the historic middle-aged skill of subtle compromise.

I started driving, when I was 12 years old, a go-kart that my brother and I put together. We grew up fairly near Silverstone motor-racing circuit and I was utterly captivated by it: the noise, the smell, the speed, the glamour. I loved the look of the cars, the width of the tyres, the gleam of the engines and the noise they made. I just loved that noise.

Our go-kart was powered by a 4-horsepower lawnmower engine, so it didn't have quite the same glamour, but we loved it. We then joined a club – I believe it was called the Anglia Junior Car Club. The club met up on Sundays and drove around improvised circuits on empty car parks. There were a lot of frustrated dads involved, frustrated because our little cars were just too small for them to get in and drive.

On one memorable occasion we congregated in the grounds of Easton Neston, then the stately home of Lord Hesketh, in Northamptonshire. We spent a glorious warm afternoon roaring around his lordship's network of private roads at speeds in excess of 28 miles an hour. I remember looking up at the dappled sun coming through the thick canopy of upper-class trees and luxuriating in the experience. I wasn't that bothered about setting a lap record, although it has to be noted that, because I was so light, when I drove the go-kart it zipped along nicely. The then teenage Lord Hesketh also had a similar car, but clearly his was tuned to the max and he pelted around, overtaking me a couple of times on each lap. I remember reading a while back that his Lordship eventually lost his driving licence for life after yet another staggering speeding fine.

One Sunday the car club visited Santa Pod drag raceway and raced our humble karts in front of a large audience. We probably reached 30 miles an hour, which must have been mildly amusing for the crowd, who had spent the day watching big, fat-tyred monsters topping over 200. While we were there I can clearly remember walking around the pit area with my brother, proudly holding my helmet and gawping at the colossally noisy dragsters. I think it might be questionable to expose a young mind to such serious American muscle cars; I couldn't think about anything else for weeks.

Then I saw *Bullitt* and I was doomed. *Bullitt* is a movie made in the late 1960s set in San Francisco and starring Steve McQueen. He plays Lieutenant Frank Bullitt. Yes, he's the ultra-cool cop who takes no prisoners, wears black roll-neck sweaters and he lives with Jacqueline Bisset in a cool house on one of those steep streets in San Francisco.

That's all good for starters, but add to this heady mix the fact that he drives a Highland Green 1968 Mustang GT 390 Fastback. Oh yes. That damn car chase made such an impression on my 13-year-old brain.

It is a wonderful bit of film-making. Even if you are not bothered by car chases, it is the one that set the bar sky high, and of course Mr McQueen did all his own stunt-driving. What a dude!

I was very lucky when, in 1997, I spent some time in San Francisco and a friend who lived there took me on a little *Bullitt* tour, following part of the route of the infamous car chase. Unfortunately, we weren't in a Highland Green 1968 Mustang GT 390 Fastback; we were in a rather battered Dodge van that could only just get up the steep hills, but it was still worth it. He even had a cassette tape of the soundtrack, which we could just about hear through the utterly knackered speakers. Marvellous.

So, I cannot deny my petrol-head roots. There is no way to explain to someone who's utterly uninterested in cars and engines what it is that fascinates so many people about them.

On my first trip to the United States in the 1980s, while staying in Los Angeles I hired a car from a company called Hollywood Rent-a-Wreck. It was very cheap and not far from where I was staying. Most of the dusty cronks they had on their lot were Japanese imports, but as the scruffy dude showed me what they had on offer, I noticed this big black slab of angry Detroit muscle behind the Portakabin, three-quarters covered in a tatty tarpaulin. I asked him if I could hire that and he laughed.

'No one ever wants to hire that piece of crap,' he said. 'Hasn't run in months.'

I flatly refused to listen to him. I wanted that car or nothing, so he and his equally surly assistant pulled the tarp off it and revealed a 1970 Dodge Challenger with a 450 Hemi under the hood.

OK, I'll explain my insistence. There were two cars

used in the legendary *Bullitt* chase sequence: the aforementioned Highland Green 1968 Mustang GT 390 Fastback, driven by Steve, and this baby, which the baddies drove. I had never seen one in real life and now I was going to rent this one for 25 bucks a day.

If they could start it.

I helped them swap the batteries. I checked the oil. One tyre was flat and I pumped it up with a stirrup pump, which took about an hour.

After a lot of faffing around, we managed to get it to go. It was the *Scrapheap Challenge* symphony, the electric starter motor whining away, straining against the compression of this great chunk of inefficient engineering for what seemed like an age. Once it started, even the two unwilling members of staff from the Hollywood Rent-a-Wreck company whooped and hollered. The sound: I cannot explain what it does. The sound is outrageous. It throbs up your spine; it's like an angry beast roaring. It must do something to a man's brain. It's what we feel like when we are being polite in mixed company but really want to shout out the C word and trash the place.

When I finally drove it out on to Sunset I don't think I had ever previously been happier when not in the company of friends, lovers or bowing at the end of a successful performance. It rumbled along the road, and when I stopped at the lights of Sunset and Vine, I hit the throttle and the whole car twisted to one side, such was the torque of the massive 7-litre engine. The thing drank petrol as if it had a fundamental right to squander a precious resource at a stupid level. I would guess 8 miles to the gallon would be a good benchmark, but the fuel gauge didn't work so it was impossible to tell. It belched out fumes, it stank, the electric windows didn't work – they were held up with wooden wedges you had to push in to stop them dropping down. The brakes were utterly atrocious. You had to really think ahead to where you wanted to stop, because it was more like a ship: it would eventually come to a halt but it needed a couple of miles. When I pulled up outside the house I was staying in, my very liberal, organic-food-eating, compact-car-driving friends were less than impressed. Everything about this car said red-neck, Republican racist to them. They could not understand why the gentle English guy they had seen on stage in London criticizing men for being sexist would want to be seen in such an aggressive, ugly lump of the past.

I drove it for a week, stopping every 20 miles or so to pump ever more gas into its copious tanks. I did burn rubber a couple of times when I took it up into the San Raphael Mountains, but on the whole I just cruised around, revelling in the low rumble the chronically inefficient motor made just to go down to the shops.

I never recovered from that experience, knowing, of course, that I couldn't have one of those cars in the UK. I had to make do with what was available.

I spent the next 20 years gradually working my way up through the ranks of the Volkswagen Golf marque, from GTi to VR6 to V6 4motion to the ultimate, the aforementioned VW R32. This car brought back memories of my rented Dodge: its engine was just too big to be sensible. Crammed into the engine compartment that any sane person would use for a small, low-emission diesel was the same engine that VW use for big trucks. A 3.something-litre V6, it had six gears, permanent four-wheel drive, big chunky tyres that were discreetly fitted into the bodywork, very hard suspension and incredibly uncomfortable rear seats – it was the most absurd car for a man with two kids. It could also easily reach 165 mph, and tell me, where are you allowed to do that on the Queen's highway?

Now, I have mentioned Jeremy Clarkson once or twice, and you may think in a negative way. Don't get me wrong. I think the man is a genius. It's just I don't want to be like him so much, I can't express it. I have met him once and he did immediately ask what car I drove. I said I couldn't believe he would really ask people that when he wasn't on camera. He took no notice of this and repeated the question. I eventually said, 'A Land Rover.'

'Has it got big fat American tyres fitted on to it?'

He didn't say exactly that, because he inserted about three expletives in the question, but I am resisting my Clarksonian instinct to swear. I grimaced, because my Land Rover does have 'Grabber All Terrain' tyres fitted, one of the reasons it's never got stuck in the mud in the various extreme locations it's been used on *Scrapheap Challenge*.

His response? 'It's a [expletive deleted] crime and only a [expletive deleted] would spoil a great British car with [expletive deleted] American tyres.'

I felt suitably admonished.

When I saw a *Top Gear* episode which featured my ultimate Golf, the R32, Jeremy Clarkson said it was the best car VW had ever made; in fact it was the best hatchback ever produced, it was fantastic and amazing and incredible and fast, and it gripped the road like (expletive deleted) on a blanket and all those things he relishes.

So, for all my chunky American tyres, I had a Clarkson classic parked on my drive, and do you know what I did, ladies and gentlemen? After one year of driving this tarmac terrorizer, after a year of spending a fortune on petrol and car insurance, I drove it to a Toyota dealer and traded it in for a Prius T Spirit hybrid petrol-electric SULEV.

Even the salesman was a little surprised when I turned up in it. I rumbled into the forecourt in my 3.2-litre Golf and I whined out in a 1.diddly-squit-litre hybrid electric front-wheel-drive Toyota tree-hugger. For a petrol-head who's cruised Sunset in a Dodge Challenger let me tell you, that's a big step.

To finish outlining Clarkson's involvement in my life, and I'd like to state now it has been minimal, he has even gone to the bother of machine-gunning a Prius to bits, he hates them so much. It's one of the reasons I've stuck with it: anything that Clarkson hates that much has got to be a good thing. I love the congestion charge, speed humps, speed cameras and the pipe dream of an efficient and cheap public transportation system. I adore road cones, bus lanes, cycle lanes, low speed limits, calming zones and blocked-off rat runs. I make a point of loving all the things he hates. I use him as a moral compass. He's a very useful man.

So for me to give up a pokey hot hatch for a prim and proper Prius has been an emotional journey. It's not been easy, but I know it had to be done. It is the same with so much of my adult experience. I can't ban cars, I can't turn motorways back into vegetable allotments, but I can drive cars that don't drink petrol. My argument is not environmental, it's about common sense. Fossil fuels are a finite resource, so why use as much as you can as fast as you can when you can achieve exactly the same thing, i.e. get from point A to point B, using much less? It's going to take another 20 years before there are truly viable affordable alternatives to fossil-fuel-powered vehicles, so I'm just trying to stretch the last few drops out a bit longer.

Finally, I just want to say the Toyota Prius is a rubbish car. It's not any more rubbish than any other car, it's only rubbish because it is a car and they are all, by definition, rubbish. Put one person in a complex metal box and create a massive infrastructure of smooth surfaces which covers tens of thousands of acres of land on a small island and then sit hundreds of individuals in hundreds of metal boxes along the length of those smooth surfaces. It doesn't matter what makes the metal boxes move along, it's a stupid system.

Shame, really, because I love driving.

That slightly damning realization aside, there are some amazing bits of automotive technology emerging around the planet that might provide an alternative to my Armageddon nightmares.

The Tesla Roadster car, developed in Silicon Valley, has caught a lot of attention lately. Backed by people with serious money who used to run things like eBay and PayPal, this little two-seater sports car goes faster than all those Porsche, Jaguar and Ferrari-type things but it doesn't use any fossil fuel to do so. It is 100 per cent electric and it costs a fortune. It's clearly designed to appeal to very rich people in America who feel a bit guilty about driving Hummers – yes, there are one or two of them – and it sounds from the reviews that it's an amazing car to drive. What's more annoying, though, is that even if I could afford to buy one, I can't. You can't buy one in this country, though, even more annoyingly, they are actually made in the UK by Lotus, in Hethel, near Norwich. I am going to have to wait until I'm in my mid-sixties before I get to drive something like this.

But let's just imagine for a moment that I could have an all-electric car which charges in a few minutes and goes 300 miles on one charge. It's still a car, it's still a metal box with one person, and where does the electricity come from? It's going to take such a huge change in our social and cultural outlook to get most people to use public transport, and there's so many of us, and we all want to move. It's very easy to give up and sit in a traffic jam listening to the radio. I am prepared to live my life weirdly in order to avoid sitting in traffic, like driving at three in the morning, but whenever I do get stuck in bad traffic I want to live under a totalitarian state with central planning and draconian regulations forcing all people to be equal. It just doesn't make sense under any political or social system to accept as a simple fact of life that 5,000 stationary people in 5,000 stationary boxes with 5,000 engines burbling away is a good idea.

However, and here's the curse for the guilt-ridden, concerned middle classes, if you tell people they can't do something you are missing a vital aspect of human nature. When someone in authority tells me I can't do something I've never thought of doing, I immediately want to do it.

I haven't driven into central London for many years simply because it's stupid and you can't park. I caught the bus, the tube, got a taxi (because I'm privileged and middle class) or, most commonly, rode my bike. I thought the introduction of the congestion charge was brilliant; at last one authority in the country was doing something about our devotion to metal-box transportation. For the first few months after it was introduced, I would say that from casual observation there really was a reduction in the number of cars driving around inside the congestion zone. However, after more careful, casual and utterly unfounded observation, I would say the type of cars you now see inside the zone has started to change, and, in my humble opinion, change for the worse. These days you generally see only big, expensive cars driven by very wealthy people. Poorer people who might need to drive in or through central London go around it. It's rich people who actually go in regularly, and they drive cars that are uniquely unsuited to a dense urban environment. If you drive a car that weighs 2 tons, costs £90,000 and achieves only 8 miles to the gallon, a car that costs you £2.50 to drive 1 mile, you are not going to be the sort of person who hesitates about a £5, £10 or even £100 congestion charge.

The change of attitude has to come from inside, from a genuine understanding of what is going on, not an imposed diktat from on high. Penalizing people makes them angry and hostile and more determined than ever to drive bigger and uglier cars that use more and more petrol to go shorter and shorter distances. The reason they want to do this is to say to 'the man', as they refer to government in the USA, 'Screw you, I'll drive what I like.' I'm not condoning that reaction, I don't admire it – it's short-sighted and self-defeating – but I do understand it.

Cheating

JULY
28
2007

'Does hiring things count? Judy and I have lived
together for 20 years, we have two children, but we
aren't married. At least we weren't until this
afternoon. Right slap bang in the middle of my year
of not shopping. The two things are in no way
connected, but it did make getting married just that
little bit extra stressful. We decided to get married
because our wonderful accountant explained it made
a lot of sense. Because we come from different sides
of the world, it just makes life easier. The kids wanted
us to get married, all our extended family members
were happy about it, it was only Judy and I who
weren't so sure.

So, we hired a big top from a local circus who
were having the year off touring, stuck it up on

the village playing field and about 130 people
we know and love turned up to celebrate. I think
everyone had a good time. I wore my new celebrity
suit and a second-hand shirt Judy bought me in a
charity shop. Amazingly, although Gloucestershire
was still half submerged in the summer floods, it was
a lovely day, bright and sunny and only mildly damp
under foot.

It didn't really feel like cheating. I didn't buy any
consumer items for the day; admittedly it cost a bomb,
but it was all hiring and renting. It's not something I
would ever do again and, maybe not surprisingly, it
seems to have made absolutely no difference to Judy or
me. We still row about the same things, the children
are still wonderfully 'challenging' and the dog still
hassles me for walks at six in the morning. I can now
legitimately describe Judy as 'my wife' and this evening
I heard her describe me as 'my husband', which I have
to say I quite like.

So I am now trying to justify this unusual expenditure
during a year of not buying anything. I can't, really,
but it was all planned long before I sulked my way
along the beach in Australia.'

I HAVE always been very good at cheating, but other than the
wedding party I haven't been able to allow myself to cheat
during my year of making do. I have made errors, but I have
never thought, 'What the hell, buy it, who's going to know?' I

am now wondering if this new-found inner strength is going to hold my resolve with cigarettes.

My watch was a good example. I have had it for years, it's one of those 'wind itself up' watches that don't have batteries and never stop working. At least it didn't until I dropped it early in the year of not shopping and it started to rattle in a new and challenging way. One of the reasons it was challenging was that it didn't tell the time: it was permanently stuck on half-past four. So I took it in to be repaired; I had allowed myself to repair things and it felt good. It felt good until the man at the repair shop said it would take about five months. He'd have to send it off to Belgium or somewhere. So I said goodbye to my trusty watch in January and it was returned to me at the beginning of June. It cost much more to fix than it would have done to buy a new watch, but that's what I did. I am wearing it now and it's perfect.

The same thing happened with shoes. I bought a pair of pull-on Australian cattleman's boots in Melbourne in 1992 and I have worn them regularly ever since. Because the heels were so worn down by the start of 2007 I kept falling over, so I took them into a repair shop and had them reheeled. I decided that repairing them wasn't cheating either. They are fine and I still wear them. I didn't think about it much, but I did feel a bit guilty. After all, the watch must have contained new parts and the heels of my boots were new. I don't know if it's truly cheating, though.

I have always been aware that the person I have cheated the most is myself, and taking a year out from consuming has shown me that it is possible to move on, to change, to stop cheating.

Cheating

One of the things I'd never really thought about until this year was newspapers. I don't buy them that often as a general rule, but just occasionally I will pick one up if I am in a position to have a luxury, child-free treat, like breakfast in a café in London. Then I will generally take my time, sipping coffee and orange juice and munching a croissant, reading through the horrors of the world in a newspaper.

On a fresh morning in July, well into my year of making do, I was due to meet my old friend Ed Bye, one-time director of *Red Dwarf* and husband of the legend that is Ruby Wax, in London. We had arranged to hook up at ten o'clock on Portobello Road. I planned to get there early and grab some breakfast.

As I walked up Westbourne Grove I passed a newsagent's and had to check myself as I totally unconsciously walked in to buy a paper. I grimaced. I knew no one would see me, no one would find out, it was the sort of cheat I had spent my life getting away with. I mostly cheat at smoking. I tell my wife and children that I have given up, I don't smoke at home, and then, on a morning such as this, I discreetly buy a packet of fags and smoke like a British Tommy in the trenches.

This time, for some reason I still haven't fully understood, I turned round and walked out. I didn't buy a paper. I didn't buy anything: fags, newspapers, chewing gum, magazines. Nothing. I had managed over six months without buying anything and it would be so stupid to blow it for a copy of the *Independent*. I felt a bit miserable as I pictured myself sitting alone, having my breakfast with nothing to read but the menu.

Then my spirits rose. We were meeting in one of those trendy restaurant/bars where they always have newspapers lying around, some of them on big poles hanging up on the wall. I didn't need to buy one; I could just read one that was already there. Basically, I could cheat.

I walked into the restaurant a few minutes later with a spring in my step. This making-do lark wasn't so hard after all. I was shown to a table and I placed my order, then I scanned the restaurant for a discarded paper. Anything, I didn't care. I'd even read the *Daily Mail*. There were no newspapers on poles hanging on the wall; there were no piles of discarded newspapers anywhere. I noticed a suited businessman reading the *Financial Times*, but when he got up to leave he took his wretched paper with him, the mean, self-made, new-monied bastard.

I cannot believe how many times I have been in a restaurant in the morning and it is festooned with newspapers, but this particular establishment was utterly newsprint-free.

What I did instead was discreetly watch the rest of the clientele, and if you ever get the chance to have breakfast on Portobello Road, it's worth not buying a newspaper and just checking out the action.

There is the usual gaggle of fashionable men with designer stubble and baggy jeans, but it's the young mums who are truly impressive. They arrive after about nine-fifteen, are always talking on their phones and will have the biggest and most impressive pushchairs you can imagine, the Porsche Cayenne of pushchairs, bigger and more rugged than could ever be necessary. One woman came in with two kids in a massive contraption that took up all available floor space. She was talking on not one but two phones at the same time, asking one phone to hold while she finished talking on the other. The staff were having to gingerly negotiate around her, carrying plates of food high up and balancing precariously as they eased around the massive form factor of the fat-tyred buggy. It was brilliant, I loved it, and the bits of conversation you overhear are utterly intriguing.

I heard names that I decided were those of the mega rich and globally famous.

'Roger said he doesn't care how much it costs, we have to get it,' is a quote I noted down at the time. I decided this Roger was probably Roger Moore, or Roger Waters from Pink Floyd. I decided that all these women were the second wives of extremely successful rock stars or actors. They were all slim and gorgeous, their hair was magnificent, the jeans they wore complemented their Cuban-heeled designer cowboy boots perfectly. These were top-end rock chicks for whom the concept of not buying anything for a year would be as alien as making your kid walk to school.

When Ed joined me he obviously knew half of them, being a long-time Notting Hill resident. I pitched my theory at him and he immediately shot it down in flames. Apparently most of these women ran their own PR companies and were married to merchant bankers.

The other newspaper event happened a couple of months later and was in some ways connected. I spent a couple of days during the making-do year working with Craig Charles, also an ex-Red Dwarfer. He told me about his most recent shenanigans and asked me not to buy the Sunday newspapers because there would be a big article about him and his new-found sober status appearing in one particularly lurid tabloid. I explained that he needn't worry, I wasn't buying anything new, including newspapers, for a whole year. Craig looked at me for a moment, trying to understand what I had just said.

'Are you broke, Bob? D'you need a few quid?' he asked, genuinely concerned.

Contrary to what a lot of people might think, I have always found Craig to be a very generous and honourable friend – he certainly looked after me when I was getting a bit wilty under rubber on the set of *Red Dwarf*.

I explained to him that it was an experiment to see how hard it was to do, that it was my emotional response to a world gone mad on consumerism, that it was a stance against the endless need for the new thing.

'Twat,' was Craig's honest-to-goodness response. He is nothing if not honest.

So, the following Sunday I woke up, looked in the fridge and saw we had no milk, a common event in our household. I jumped in the Land Rover with the big American (expletive deleted) tyres and drove 3 miles down the hill to the nearest open shop. We do have a village shop much nearer, but it is run by volunteers, one of them being me, and it doesn't open until ten in the morning. I bought some milk and saw Craig's face looming out from the papers piled in neat rows near the door.

'Oh, and this please,' I said, putting the paper with the milk without a second thought. I wanted to see what Craig had said in the interview and it looked fairly chunky. I drove back up the hill, opened the front door and there on the mat was another copy of exactly the same paper.

I asked Judy where it had come from. She explained that a neighbour of ours had bought it for me, knowing I wasn't buying anything and thinking I would like to read it.

It was like being punched in the stomach. I cursed myself for having bought the damn thing. Although it didn't matter to anyone else, it really mattered to me. Not only that, our neighbour, Deirdre, who is not someone I would naturally agree with politically, was so kind and generous that she had gone to the bother of buying the paper for me. I felt like a heel.

So, OK, it wasn't strictly speaking cheating, it was a momentary lapse, but I took it as a stark reminder. It actually galvanized me to really make an effort, to tighten the straps and not allow myself to buy anything other than food and medicine.

A great many people who knew about what I was trying to do suggested that Judy could buy things for me and allow me to get around my absurd, self-imposed restrictions without cheating. I tried to explain that this made the whole thing pointless.

I have to say, though, that Judy did get me one new pair of trousers for my birthday. 'I can't walk down the street with you wearing those bloody awful things,' was her reasoning. This was said during a birthday treat for me when we went to Amsterdam for two days without the kids. We had both performed in the city when we were young, carefree comedians and we spent a day wandering about trying to find our old haunts.

After a visit to the Anne Frank house, a place neither of us had been to before, Judy agreed to record a YouTube piece for me while we were standing on a bridge over the canal on the Prinzengracht. It was during this process that she panned the camera down to show the state of my strides. She said they were embarrassing and she was right. Later that day I did go into a shop with her and we bought a pair of new, off-the-peg, probably made-in-China trousers. I found it quite painful, it did feel like cheating and I did have plenty of pairs of trousers, but they were all worn, patched, stained and saggy.

Then there was the suit. Now, this is complicated and could make it sound like I live the life of a proper celebrity who people have heard of, rather than 'that bloke who's on that thing', which is how I am mostly described. The suit was a complete turn-up for me, a first, a truly magic moment. During the year before I made my decision I was contacted by a tailor called Brad Green with premises on London's Savile Row. He asked me if I was prepared to be given a free made-to-measure suit. I would love to be able to claim that, as a minor low-grade celeb who gets recognized in petrol filling stations across the land by blokes in white vans, I am constantly bombarded with offers like this and I just pass them to my people to deal with. Sadly, that is very far from the case. I have never been given anything other than a peaked cap with the image of a digger on the front, so this was a bit of a thrill. Although I was a little concerned there must be a catch and I would soon see embarrassing pictures of myself in *Suits You* monthly, when I met the charming Mr Green I was put at ease. He makes one suit a year for a celebrity, as it has proved to be very good publicity. In the past he has done numerous chaps you might have heard of, but I don't feel it polite to name them. I felt very puffed up until he gently informed me that he wasn't even sure who I was, but his fiancée was a big *Red Dwarf* fan and she had told him to get in touch. He'd never even watched *Red Dwarf*, likewise *Scrapheap Challenge*, so as I stood there being measured I was slightly deflated, which possibly gave rise to a false set of measurements.

A few months later and well into my making-do year I returned to his premises and tried the suit on. It was amazing. It fitted beautifully and made me stand up straight. It's a three-piece, very muted dark brown pinstripe, nicely balanced with a slightly flashy, showbiz blue silk lining. I am very lucky to have it and I also promised myself, and the charming tailor, that when my year was up I would buy another one. Check the chapter 'Final Irony' to find out why this was not to be.

So I think that is the sum total of major cheats of the year. The other ones are subtler. I subscribe to a magazine called *Wired* and the subscription started in November, which meant I received a copy every month. I suppose I could have cancelled it, but as it had already been paid for and I couldn't be bothered to go through the hassle, I left it. I did therefore have ample reading material through the year and have just been through the enormous hassle of resubscribing after my year was up.

Another thing was books. I do read a lot of books, but one thing I discovered was that I buy even more. It would have been a couple of months into the year when I went through the overstacked bookshelves in our house and dug out over a dozen books I had bought previously, sometimes years previously, and never read. At the end of the year I still hadn't finished all of them, which just goes to show the dangers of

Radio 4 or podcasts and an open laptop with a wireless
Internet connection when you are cooking. I hear Melvin
Bragg or Andrew Marr mention some weird book and I go to
Amazon and instantly buy it with one click.

Breaking that habit has been a positive benefit. I haven't
reverted to it since I stopped making do, and although it may
affect Amazon's bottom line, it does mean I will finish all the
books I have already before I buy any more.

Cheap Stuff

AUG
17
2007

'OK, now this is all getting really difficult. It's not
big things that I'm missing buying, it's tiny things.
I have sewn up the holes in my socks. I have patched
my favourite trousers. I have fixed the puncture on my
26-year-old bicycle. It's not that I truly need any of
these things replaced with new stuff, it would just
be so much easier. I never thought I would live to see
the day that I became depressed when I opened my
sock drawer, but I did this morning. It's just tragic. I've
also become increasingly worried about money.
There's nothing to cheer me up, it's all gone very drab.'

AT THE time of writing, in the developed world, generally
speaking, stuff is cheap. It's never been cheaper; consuming
stuff we don't need is so easy it's embarrassing. In terms of
hours worked, as opposed to actual amounts of money, the

time it took someone to earn enough to buy a mobile phone when they were first introduced in the late 1970s and the time it takes now is a very good example. When the movie *Wall Street*, starring Michael Douglas and Charlie Sheen, was released, a mobile phone was a big brick of a thing that cost 460 work hours for someone on the average wage at the time. Today you can get a much better, much smaller, much more efficient phone for less than three hours' work.

Using the same way of measuring, clothing is a staggering 62 per cent cheaper than 30 years ago, cars are a mind-numbing 70 per cent cheaper and, most impressively, food is a full 87 per cent cheaper than it was in 1978. Isn't that incredible? Hard to believe? Absurd? I think so, but I also think I am probably wrong in doing so.

Surely this is brilliant. This is the future. This is development and modern life and excitement and possibility all rolled into one big spend-a-thon. Stuff has got cheaper; we don't have to work as hard to be able to buy as much as we did 30 years ago. We have done it: we have made the world the way we want it. We can have more leisure time and help rear our children better. We can build better communities and be more creative because we can feed, dress and house ourselves for so much less work time than we used to be able to.

Any of this ringing true to you?

No, I didn't think so. So what has happened?

Why is it that over the past ten years so many people seem to have had so much money to spend on overseas holidays, cars, flat-screen TVs, mobile phones and iPods? I'm sure an economist or the Chancellor of the Exchequer could come up with a plethora of reasons, but I think one of the most obvious can be found when you walk around a supermarket.

To put it plainly, food, the most important consumer commodity there is, is dead cheap. I've done a bit of research but it's brief, so bear with me. In 1949 the average family spent 26 per cent of its annual income on food. In 2007 the figure's around 9 per cent. It is as simple as that, there is no mystery. Food, the one thing we all truly need, is very cheap and we've all got used to it.

I can remember a few years ago there was still some resistance from small shop-keepers, people like butchers and greengrocers, to the ever-expanding dominance of the big supermarket chains. I can't remember the last time I heard those arguments on a food programme on Radio 4, or read an article about a greengrocer going out of business in Richmond because the old gasworks had been demolished and replaced by a giant Tesco. It's certainly been a while.

The supermarkets have won. There is no alternative if you live in a city; there's pitifully little alternative if you live in a village, believe me.

It's true that farmers' markets have appeared over the last few years, but if you look at the picture at a national level, they account for only a tiny fraction of the food consumed in this country.

The number of shops on farms has increased over the last few years. These have changed the face of the countryside and do offer some sort of alternative to the ubiquitous supermarket, but it's still a small drop in a very large ocean.

However, there is a farm shop a few miles from where I live which stands out from the crowd and may be pointing to the future. Boy, does it stand out. It is an extraordinary place called Daylesford and it is becoming legendary.

It is essentially a farm shop, as it is a shop – though maybe I should use the term 'store', because it's very big – and it is on a farm. A real, proper farm with tractors and cows and barns and fields and sheep. If you now have the mental picture of a rustic farm with dilapidated buildings, piles of muck and knackered old gates, erase those images permanently. Daylesford is very, very smart. It's financed by the Bamford family, who originally developed the JCB digger. Lady Bamford has invested serious amounts of money into this venture and to call Daylesford a farm shop is to undersell it horribly. Lady Bamford would be mortified; I apologize, your ladyshipness.

There is no simple way of describing Daylesford, but let me put it like this. Ever been to Harrods food hall in Knightsbridge? Well, Daylesford makes that look like a run-down branch of Iceland in a deprived housing estate in the north-east of England. The vast majority of what Daylesford sells is grown on their own farm, and it's a very beautiful farm, set in the gently rolling Cotswold Hills between Chipping Norton and Stow-on-the-Wold. Yes, the Cotswolds, where all the film stars and rock stars are supposed to live, if you read the *Daily Mail*, or where an enormous number of merchant bankers live if you are actually here. Oh, and I suppose I should say the odd scruffy comedian/actor/TV presenter/writer happens to live in the area too.

The food they produce and sell at Daylesford is all organic, obviously, but far more importantly it all comes from their own farms. The meat they sell is from their own animals in the fields surrounding the shop or from their large livestock farm in Staffordshire. The animals are all free-range and reared in a sustainable way. The milk they produce from their dairy herd is used to make their now world-renowned cheese. They also stock the cheese that the bloke from Blur makes; yes, it's that hip. The bakery that is on the premises uses locally sourced flour and the bread is wonderful. It's all wonderful – they don't sell anything that's a bit rubbish, it's all fantastic.

Now, let me just explain for those of you who have never heard of Daylesford Farm shop, darling, you haven't lived. Daylesford is posh, it's staggeringly expensive, the cars that crunch over the thick gravel car park are from an exclusive line of vehicles that include Aston Martin, Bentley, Rolls-Royce and Range Rover, although I did see a rather brash-coloured Ferrari there once. Weekender, darling, new money.

That is, of course, unless we visit in our knackered old van, which I think says something brave and arty about our delightful bohemian attitude to life.

Daylesford is very fashionable. Apparently it's constantly packed with celebs, although I can honestly say every time I've been there I haven't seen anyone famous. In fact, I can show off and say that I have always been the most famous person there when I've been. The staff recognize me and smile. They say, 'Hello, Robert, how are you?'

OK, OK, one member of staff is a friend's son, so it's not really anything to do with celebrity status. Anyway, those thin women who, I'm told, appear in magazines like *Heat*, *Hello!* and *OK!* shop there all the time, the local Daylesford wives tell me.

It's wonderfully staffed: there are a lot of them, they are all slim and healthy, and they all wear beige and look like they've just walked out of a 1990s Benetton advert. Every race on earth is represented behind the wonderful cheese counter and yet Daylesford is in the middle of nowhere. The nearest town is Stow-on-the-Wold, for goodness' sake, and that is full to the gunnels with gay antique dealers. The racial mix in this part of the world is resolutely monocultural, so I don't know where this multinational sales force actually lives. Possibly in an exquisitely converted medieval barn somewhere on the estate.

However, what I feel Daylesford represents is what food would cost if it were to be produced in a way that was traditional old-school, which means, ironically, truly sustainable. They sell food that is produced in a way that doesn't rely on massive EC subsidies and the devastating overuse of multinational-controlled pesticides and copyrighted suicide seeds. The fact that Daylesford is posh and fashionable is really a side issue that all the clever and knowing journalists who've written reviews about it have missed.

What Daylesford produces and sells is, without question, better than anything you can buy in a supermarket; not just better-tasting and better for you, but produced with minimum carbon footprint and minimum damage to the land. If my family shopped there exclusively, and we just about could in terms of the range of products they have on offer, we would spend a massively increased proportion of our income on food, probably something close to the 1949 level of 26 per cent. Oddly enough, everyone around us, everyone who has ever been to Daylesford, would think we were mad, wildly extravagant or just being un-British and showing off. But we would only be spending 26 per cent of our income on food, just like everyone did 60 years ago, and, boy, would we eat well.

I once actually bought a Daylesford steak. I don't eat much red meat anyway and this was a special treat. It cost about £14, for one steak. It wasn't even that big, but it was fantastic. I really appreciated it. I didn't wolf it down without thinking. Instead, I took my time eating it, and, man, that baby melted in the mouth.

So, how on earth can I suggest that ordinary members of the public change their shopping habits and start spending vast sums at emporia like Daylesford? You can occasionally see ordinary members of the public wandering around the Daylesford rural-lifestyle complex, looking a bit dazed and intimidated. My children cannot stand the place and have frequently embarrassed me by picking up a lavender sack about the right size for a Barbie doll and proclaiming loudly, 'Dad, look at this. It's £40!' Another time my daughter picked up a silver pizza cutter and waved it at me from the other side of the busy store. 'Dad, this one is £120!' I smiled awkwardly and walked over to see her and ask her not to be quite so loud, assuming it was £12 and she had read the label incorrectly. I looked at the pizza cutter, nice wooden handle, little cutty wheel thing, and she was right. There on the price tag: £120. Blimey.

That aside, if you buy their fruit and veg, which are obviously seasonal – they are not flying in Kenyan beans all year round – it is barely more expensive than at the Stow branch of Tesco up the road.

Seasonal food, not exactly a revolutionary idea. Reminds me of my mum again. I have seen black-and-white pictures of the middle of Cheltenham taken by her during the war. Every park is an allotment, every garden dug over and growing vegetables. People grew stuff alongside railway lines. They had to, because there wasn't going to be anything to eat if they didn't.

Obviously, buying food from somewhere like Daylesford is an absurd luxury, but the cost of the produce there genuinely reflects what it would cost to feed ourselves rather than import it all.

It's the same as the Paul Smith T-shirt for £90 as opposed to the supermarket one for £3. It just feels to me that Daylesford is realistic and Tesco, Sainsbury, Budgens et al. are living in a fantasy land of borrowed time and money, utterly reliant on stable global trade and endless fossil fuel reserves.

There is another farm shop, a proper one in a battered old shed, which is much nearer our house and I have to say I much prefer going there. Hayles Fruit Farm shop also sells locally produced food and, obviously, because of that the range varies throughout the year. Seasonal availability is something I grew up with but it has virtually disappeared for most of us. Our local farm shop is a good reminder of what seasonal really means.

The shop part of the business is actually on a fruit farm – they grow raspberries, strawberries, apples and pears. If you go there in February they won't have many of these on display, but they do have potatoes, wonderful local ham, root vegetables and the best apple juice you can buy. During the spring they have asparagus, and the best meal of the year in our house is their ham, asparagus and new potatoes. Absolutely simple: steam the spuds and asparagus, slap out the ham on a plate, add a bit of butter, job done.

So here I am with my Armageddon fears about the collapse of the global transportation system and the sudden increase in the price of food, and the sudden and catastrophic decrease in its abundance and availability. It is such a fragile system.

During the floods of 2006, which affected our local area a great deal (not us, I might add, as we are very lucky to live on the Cotswold escarpment, about 600 feet above sea level; if we get flooded we are likely to see an ark float past just before we sink beneath the waves), none of the local shops had any milk or bread or bog roll. The trucks couldn't get through. People panicked and bought more than they needed, and yet you only needed to go 5 miles in the other direction and there were ample supplies.

We like to have a panic; I started screaming in the shop when there wasn't any bog roll, people queued up to buy bottles of water, gallons of water in plastic bottles. Total instant panic due to a dreadful amount of local flooding and the news reports, but it was local, it wasn't national. There was somewhere to go to get bog roll, any shop a few miles up the road. Imagine if there was nowhere. Maybe I am focusing on the bog roll situation a little too much; what about bread and milk? No, for me it is always the fear of running out of bog roll.

Simply increase the impact those floods had to a national or even international level. Most of the food we eat is imported; if those imports stopped, what would we do? Martin Adams, a local farmer we know – yes, he really is a farmer, although most of his barns have been converted to holiday lets – has a fairly sardonic view of the food industry. I want to describe Martin accurately because I know many people in towns think of farmers as members of the land-owning gentry, both huge houses and thousands of acres of private land surrounding them. While I am sure there are plenty of farmers like this, Martin isn't one of them. His dad still drives a tractor around the place and his son works there too. They are not in the least posh; they are very kind and gentle people with a great sense of humour. Well, maybe not about supermarkets.

The supermarkets have such an iron grip on the market there is no alternative for the farmers but to sell to them. The supermarkets have all the cards. If Martin can't go anywhere else to sell his stuff, he can't negotiate and they beat him down to the absolute lowest possible price.

I stood in one of his fields with him on a lovely summer's evening a couple of years back as we watched his herd of beef cattle munch the thick grass. I asked him what would happen if the world ran out of oil and all the imports stopped. He chuckled; clearly this tickled him a bit. He said the buyer from Tesco would come round and say, 'We want to buy all the beef you've got right now.' Martin said he would reply, 'Right, well, let me tell you how much that's going to cost *you*.' His dream is to have the wellie on the other foot, to be able to dictate the price of his produce to the supermarket buyers rather than the other way round, and that sentiment isn't going to go away.

'The children are back at school after a long summer holiday. It's been a very difficult holiday because of the complex arrangements for their education. My daughter is at a private school, my son at a state school. The story behind that is so long and complex, so painful and confusing, I don't think I will ever understand it. The very fact that I have ever paid for my children to be privately educated has left me somewhat bedraggled. It was never something I even thought about before I had children, but over this particular summer holiday, it's something I have been unable to forget.'

I HAVE used the term 'middle class' many times so far – too many times, I admit. Class has been a life-long obsession of mine, for which I have often been criticized. I apologize, because it is an uncomfortable subject, but claim the right to continue to use the term ad nauseam.

I hadn't thought about class for years. It's not really an issue any more, is it? Maybe race, fundamentalism and climate change have moved class completely off the agenda. However, not going shopping for one year has made me aware of the British class system for the first time in decades and, again, this wasn't something I had considered when I started.

As a child I was very aware of it. It was part of the world I grew up in. My mother was from a fairly well-to-do middle-class family. Her father ran a piano shop on the Promenade in Cheltenham and they even had a maid when she was a little girl. My father came from a working-class family. He grew up in a council house and his dad delivered milk from a horse-drawn milk float.

It was possibly this mixing of the classes which, from observing the way my mother referred to my father and his background, made me more than generally aware of what it all meant. My mother wasn't officially a snob, she would have refuted that accusation forcefully, but when we were on holiday she didn't like sitting on a beach next to, as she would describe them, 'the noisy hordes', which was code for 'ghastly working-class people'. If my brother and I ever slipped into our local regional accent, or anything other than standard received-pronunciation BBC English, we would be severely chastised.

In my teens I rebelled against it, obviously I did. You had to – it was just plain silly. To judge people because of their accent or dress code was pointless and all the time I met people who challenged my class assumptions. However, I would be the first to state that class-consciousness was very well entrenched in the British until, of all people, Mrs Thatcher.

I believe she did more to remove it than any left-leaning leader or fiery trade unionist in previous times. She couldn't stand the ghastly workers, but she also hated the silver-spooned posh civil servants who assumed their privileges as a birthright.

Having made that possibly rash statement, the jolly old class system is still with us.

The very act of making do for a year has forced me to accept finally that I am middle class, not even lower or upper middle class, just dull old middle middle class. That is such a boring thing to be and I am not proud.

OK, so I am going to generalize now, and make more rash, outlandish claims that have nothing to back them up. Personally, I'm looking forward to it, so here goes.

Middle-middle-class people worry and fret and writhe about with guilt and anxiety about the most stupid things. Middle-middle-class people don't have much fun. We internally criticize and judge other people, especially people from other classes, but we rarely express these feelings publicly and are totally twisted with insecurities about our own behaviour. Our every action is brimming with self-doubt, self-criticism and futile self-analysis.

Most of the working-class people I've been in contact with don't give a stuff about such matters. They have always had to live in the least pleasant places with the least money, near the busy road, the factory, the runway approach, the train line, the waste tip, the slag heap, the power station or the pylon.

They don't care about the environment or recycling for very good reasons – they want to consume more, loads more, they don't want to ponce about making do, and why should they?

For hundreds of years, generation after generation, they've had to make do with next to nothing, while at the same time being aware that the few people who were really rich didn't give a fart about them. Even with my rash generalizations, I want to point out I am not talking about unemployed or homeless people here. The working class are people with jobs who have mortgages and go on foreign holidays; they want new product purchases and designer labels.

Then there are the upper classes. Not that many of them, I'll grant you, but they are still around and they still own most of the land. The mistake many people make about the upper classes, people who talk posh and wear a lot of brown, is that they are rich. Their wealth has nothing to do with it, whereas history has everything to do with it. I have known a few renegade members of the upper classes over the years and they have generally been penniless, they have always smoked and drunk fairly heavily and they have always got on swimmingly well with working-class people. I don't mean they invite them to dinner or grand house parties, but they have no qualms or guilt when dealing with them. They accept the status quo and don't want to do anything to change it.

By contrast, any interaction between middle-class and working-class people is riddled with anxiety, guilt, fear, mistrust and snobbish judgements about taste, dress codes and eating habits.

Middle-class people like myself might often have more money than upper-class people, but we feel guilty about it.

I had to make do as a special year-long project; upper-class people have always made do with what they are born with, which just happens to be more than the rest of us can ever imagine having.

Yet again, I am making crass generalizations here – something I love to do and am often severely criticized for. But stay with me for a while. I know I am being general; in fact I can already hear you citing the numerous examples of working-class people who don't buy into consumer culture, middle-class people who strike out and find an alternative method of living, upper-class people who spend their lives and energy helping others.

Yes, accepted, all that is true. But ...

Walk around any shopping mall on any weekday and observe what is going on. Drive through any recently built housing estate and take notes. The generalizations I am making are built on hard evidence. Working-class people will generally have more new stuff and want to live in newer houses than middle-class people, and upper-class people will have the oldest stuff by a few thousand years.

There was one period in my early life when the class system was explained to me in great detail as if by the hand of the Lord. I shared a small flat in Oxford at a later period than the one covered in my *Thin He Was and Filthy-haired* book. There were three of us in the place, Piers, me and Sid: upper, middle and lower class perfectly personified. I cannot tell you the amount of sitcoms I have tried to write based on this relatively short episode in my life. I have had more rejection letters than you'd think a sane person could deal with; maybe there's a clue in that last statement.

There's no point denying it, we broke through the class barriers and shared a house together because of the length of our hair, our class-transcending taste in music and our penchant for smoking marijuana.

However, old entrenched values were only wallpapered over by our affiliation with the counterculture. Piers and Sid had a natural in-built ability not to worry about anything, including eating, clearing up, earning money and making sure there was bog roll in the loo. I, on the other hand, worried constantly.

I would come back from my damp, cold leather-craft workshop and say, 'Man, we've got no food, it's a total downer,' as I looked at the two recumbent young men sprawled on bean bags listening to Piers's totally cool Bang & Olufsen, which his dad had bought him. The subtext of what I was saying was, 'I am the only one who has ever cooked anything, ever bought any bread and milk, ever cleared up, ever done the laundry, ever moved the rubbish off the narrow flight of stairs since we've lived here.'

On the other hand, Piers supplied the sound system and the cool friends who'd drop by, and Sid supplied the limitless drugs.

It was a total waste of time me moaning. They were always so stoned it's doubtful they would have heard anything, main text or subtext.

I was further put out because I felt closer in class terms to Piers and yet he seemed to prefer Sid's company. Piers was a master of inactivity; he could sit around listening to Yes and Barclay James Harvest for literally months at a stretch. Sid could sleep for England.

It made me realize that I could never truly enter either world, and I tried, believe me. I have tried adopting cockney accents to sound well hard. I have tried imitating posh accents to sound seriously minted. I have always failed and ended up back in the middle.

We are all still trapped by it in this country. The only way you can really move from one class to another is by breeding. As an individual you have no hope; it takes generations to shift. The old cliché 'Generate, accumulate, dissipate', describing the actions of three generations of one family, has been alarmingly verified on so many occasions in my experience. Rough tough bloke clambers out of the gutter and makes a pile; he generates. He educates his son – let's be honest here, not his daughter – the son takes over the business, having been bought up in hardship, and is equally driven to accumulate. In turn his son is educated to a greater degree. His son has not known hardship; far from it, he's known nothing but luxury from day one. He inherits a big chunk of property and cash and lives the life of Riley, basically chain-smoking, getting pissed and not looking after his children very well. There may well be further terms to add to the list for future generations, where some great-great-grandson descendant of the original generator starts again, but basically that's how it goes.

I think there is one other thing that has knocked the corners off the class system in this country in the last 40 years: immigration. As class-obsessed Anglo-Saxons, we can't place people from other countries. It's most vexing. Living with an Australian, I have become very aware of this. There is no real class clue to be had from an Australian accent, but most middle- and upper-class people assume all Australians are working class. Let me say right now that this isn't always the case, or is that already obvious?

I only truly became aware of just how much we are trapped in a class system when I first escaped our wonderful shores. Actually it wasn't until I escaped the European Union, as other European countries have a long history too, and the remnants of class systems, and they also speak difficult-to-learn languages which made understanding what was going on very hard for me.

But America was a revelation. After a couple of months in the USA when I was in my early thirties I realized that no one knew if I was middle class or not. Not only did they not know as soon as I opened my mouth, they didn't care. They might care if I was rich or poor, violent or stupid, but they didn't even know what a class system as we understand it was. The lucky so-and-sos.

I was at a party in Los Angeles and I loved it, mainly because I was getting a lot of attention from a noisy group of alarmingly attractive young women. This wasn't like some scene from a teen comedy film where all the girls are blonde airheads who scream and giggle. These were tough, worldly, highly astute women with powerful media careers and a good grounding in world affairs. However, their weakness for a man with a British accent became immediately apparent. They loved the way I spoke; one of them said she thought I sounded just like Prince Andrew.

No one would ever have said that in Old England; they would have been able to tell the difference in seconds. Our ears are very finely tuned to the nuance of a British class accent. We can instantly tell when someone is trying to put on a fake accent and we would judge them harshly.

I have even met people who can pin down your origins to within a few square miles, most notably Joan Washington, who is one of the leading voice coaches in the country. I only worked with her for one day, on *Grushko*, the BBC series made in Russia I mentioned earlier. All the actors had to have a bit of coaching in how to do a subtle Russian accent, all dark Ls and rounded Rs. We sat around a big table reading out excerpts from the script and as we did so Joan would listen to each actor in turn and say, 'Tyne and Wear', 'Dorset' or, in my case, 'west Oxfordshire'.

I was quite upset. I didn't think I had a west Oxfordshire accent – that's the accent Pam Ayers has. I attended the same school as her but I don't sound like her, do I?

Joan Washington has a super-developed ear. She has voice-coached just about every famous actor you've ever seen in movies as diverse as *Star Wars*, *Captain Corelli's Mandolin* and, more recently, *Elizabeth*.

She not only has a good ear, but can do any regional British accent you care to mention utterly convincingly. She has to be good if she is going to teach an American or Australian how to sound English; the vast majority of the potential British audience will pick up on a mistaken vowel sound without even trying.

So there I was in Los Angeles, suddenly liberated from all this baggage, in a big house at a party surrounded by women who seemed interested in me just because of my accent. When told I sounded like Prince Andrew, I smiled and maybe even said something like 'How charming', which I would never say in this country. Another woman asked if I knew Prince Andrew (I imagine Andy was in the press a lot at the time, I don't recall). Anyway, without hesitation I said I didn't know him personally but we had attended the same school. This, I casually surmised, might explain the similarity in our accents. This massive, uncalled-for lie went down a storm. 'Oh, my God, you went to the same school as Prince Andrew! That is so awesome.'

I would like to point out right now that this disgraceful mistruth did not land me in a sweaty pit of carnal activity, as I had no doubt desired. I returned home in the rear seat of a compact squashed by a child seat and a pile of groceries, but it was worth a punt.

Being middle middle class is complicated. You never quite fit in anywhere other than the dull world of the middle middle class. I can see now that I struggled with all my might for many years to throw off this mundane yoke and failed utterly.

Another lesson I learned in my youth was the error of trying to appear to be above your station, as my granny would have said. In my early twenties, for reasons that have now escaped me, I fell in with a social group of quite extreme poshness. I think it was through my girlfriend at the time, who, although from Manchester, was from the posh side of town and went to a posh school where she mixed with posh girls. We went to parties where these posh friends all stood around and chain-smoked Cocktail Sobranie cigarettes. These came in posh packets and each one was rolled in different-coloured paper. They also drank cocktails and knew what they were called. They wore scruffy second-hand clothes they'd no doubt scavenged off their grandparents –

clothes which had clearly been the height of fashion in the 1920s (this was a very popular look at the time). The men all wore baggy suits they would have pinched from a dead uncle's dressing room, while the women wore original 1920s cocktail frocks which fell off their shoulders alluringly. I would have been wearing a pair of brown leather goof boots I had made myself, my long hair would have been in a ponytail down to my ass and I'd be sporting a pair of jeans decorated with embroidered Celtic knots. Not quite the same look and, when I think back now, I must have had balls. I must have stood out like a Palestinian grocer at a barmitzvah, but I didn't care, much.

One of the advantages I have always had is a good ear for accents. I could sound just like them, but it was obvious even to me that they knew I wasn't one of them. I am not saying they treated me badly, they were anything but snobbish, but they had a languorous attitude to life that can only come from the knowledge that if the proverbial really hits the fan, Daddy, Mummy or the trust fund will see you through. I would be standing at the party knowing that if the proverbial really hit my fan, I had £14.27 in a building society savings account and I had lost the account book.

One particular party was held in a spacious London apartment belonging to Lord and Lady something or other – it really was, I saw an invitation for them on the mantelpiece: 'The Archduke of somewhere requests the company of Lord and Lady something or other.' Can't remember any of the names now and thankfully his lordship and ladyness weren't present. They would have been at the country house, I suppose.

I stood around not really fitting in and this is when the whole charade finally got to me. I wanted to be as relaxed and debauched as these people, to live without a care in the world, but I knew I couldn't. I had to go to work the next day and worry and save and care about everything. I had tried to fit in, to be like them, even to sound like them, and I had failed miserably. I was living a lie and it was too painful to go on.

Whereas previously I had always tried to blend in, I decided to go to the other extreme, to try and appear slightly dangerous and very working class. I was living in Bermondsey at the time, in an old warehouse on the River Thames. The local people who lived in the area had very strong London accents that I had enjoyed listening to and I'd been carefully practising imitating. The actor Michael Caine comes from this ancient part of south London, or, in the local parlance, 'sarf Lannunn'.

I swigged from a bottle of wine and noticed a very pale young woman staring at me. She introduced herself, she was a Hermione or a Geraldine, I can't remember now. I said, 'I'm well miffed wiv all the ponces at this gaff. Fancy comin' back to mine, darlin?'

This Hermione girl was utterly enthralled and stared at me adoringly. The penny dropped. Being a middle-middle-class person was just so utterly dull, darling; being a bit of rough was terribly exciting. I have to point out yet again that nothing happened, although I do seem to remember going on a date with this rather fey girl a few weeks later. She will have married someone from her own class by now and probably lives up the road from me in some massive estate with a mile-long private drive.

To put it in some historical context, the ruling elite and the lumpen peasant masses have lived side by side in this country since before recorded history. I saw it with Piers and Sid in Oxford, I see it all the time in rural Gloucestershire and it must be the reason we have had more Conservative governments and maintained the royal family throughout the last hundred years of social upheaval. They found a way of coexisting and supporting each other in their respective positions from before the Norman invasion.

As I mentioned, the best example of this is in attitudes to the British royal family. The Silver Jubilee celebrations of 1977 are still burned into my republican mind, the street parties, the flags everywhere, the big ceremonial events. Being a radical anti-monarchist, middle-class hippie, the whole thing seemed like a nonsense to me. But the upper classes loved it, of course they did. She was the Queen of England, the monarch, the last bastion of the old school. And the working classes lapped it up, of course they did. She was the Queen, she was what England was all about – bit of nationalism, know your place, have a knees-up, flags and bunting everywhere, she's a lovely lady. Only the moaning, whingeing middle classes complained and droned on about it. Oh, and the Sex Pistols of course.

The middle classes are interlopers, people who have ideas above their station, people who want to change things, mess everything up. You can hear it from either end of the social spectrum: 'Everything was fine until you lot came along.' This can be said in either the plummiest of posh accents, or any regional working-class dialect you care to pick. The middle classes messed it up, grew bigger and more influential, took over more and more institutions, and the Old England the middle classes still long for has been subsumed forever.

Being middle class is now seen as normal. Shops, newspaper sales, advertising on TV and every other measure of social change would support this argument.

Mrs Thatcher really did her best to enforce a middle-class life on everyone, and by that I mean conservative with a small c. Look after yourself, own your house, get into debt and support the banking system. That's essentially what most of us do, and we don't riot and only complain in a whingeing, disorganized way about tax and speed cameras. When was the last time you saw a mass of mortgage payers having a demonstration and demanding changes in the way the country is run? It's not going to happen.

It did used to happen, people did make a fuss and demonstrate all the time, but Mrs Thatcher didn't care. She was prepared and if you were working class in the 1980s you got well and truly duffed up, the miners being the most obvious example. But I think what many people don't realize is that the ruling elite got a bit of a hammering too. Mrs Thatcher was a solid, hard-working lower-middle-class girl from the East Midlands. She wasn't going to be impressed by some toff who went to the right school. She savaged the old-school dominance in the civil service, she pounded the upper-class liberal 'do-gooders'. And as for posh arty homosexuals like Sir Anthony Blunt, well, look what happened to him.

So, if the whole country becomes middle class, is that a good thing? Will we be more like Sweden or Denmark? I don't really know. We are almost unable to remember what the social set-up was like before Thatcher. I can only just recall those times and I was there.

I don't feel as intimidated by posh people any more, but that might just be due to age. I know I was in awe of them as a young man, even more so as a child.

When I was at primary school I sometimes went to parties at the houses of friends who went to different schools, private ones with funny uniforms. Their houses not only smelt differently, of wood polish and damp dogs, they even had different rooms from my childhood home. They had pantries, drawing rooms, studies, parlours, staff entrances and, in one case, a moat. When your house has a moat, that's got to be something special, hasn't it? I just heard the other night, when this came up in polite conversation in the Cotswolds, that there is a big house not that far from us which has two moats. I like that. I want to hear the conversation between the family I knew who had one moat and the family up the road who have two.

'Dreadful bind, the moat, always having to clear the weeds and such.'

'Oh, goodness, we have two of the blessed things. It's such a responsibility. People without moats simply don't understand.'

These people didn't have breakfast, dinner and tea like I did, they had breakfast, lunch and dinner. They had huge gardens and indoor swimming pools, with helicopter landing pads in the orchard. They knew the history of their houses, the fact that the place was once a Royalist stronghold in the Civil War, or was the house that inspired Evelyn Waugh when he wrote *Brideshead Revisited*.

My childhood home was built in the 1930s, had pebble-dash walls and the nearest we came to a moat was the pond lined with a plastic sheet that my mum had made. I knew those people were different and I suspect I felt they were better than me. I felt embarrassed by my mum and dad when they came to pick me up. Their car was a Ford, while these people would have a Humber or a Jaguar or, in one case, a real Rolls-Royce.

But I also went to parties at the homes of children whose fathers were farm labourers and here I experienced a completely different reaction. I thought they were a bit rough and crude. Their houses were smaller than ours and smelt of wood smoke, wet dogs again – that was *de rigueur* – but also damp and old cabbage.

I suppose the reason why all these memories and ideas came floating back during my year of non-consumerism is that consumerism is the one defining activity of the middle class. But some of us are worrying about it. I don't believe the working classes are that bothered – they're all consuming like mad, no problem – but when some uppity middle-class whinger like me starts making a fuss, well, who knows where it will lead. We consume – it's almost our job. If we didn't do it what would happen to the economy? We borrow more money, we keep the banks going, we have pensions and pay for life insurance (that's another huge industry supported). Middle-class people do more shopping than anyone else. Middle-class people aren't showy, but we do want to subtly display our achievements. We don't want to crow about it – that would be too lower middle class or, heaven forbid, new-money working class. A nice Audi estate rather than a flashy Subaru Impreza with a big exhaust pipe is fine.

Our neighbours in the Cotswolds are fairly traditional posh people. They are not extravagantly rich, but they have a double-barrelled name, the husband attended Eton, while the wife's dad was a lord. The thing is, they make do by default. They are anything but snobs and have been the most wonderful neighbours. We are often looking after their chickens, ducks, ponies and dogs, and know we can call on them to do the same for us at any time. (We only have chickens and a dog.)

Their house is delightfully untidy and not festooned with new things; in fact I don't think they own anything new. All their cars are second-hand, most of their clothes too, they attend jumble sales, buy their chickens and ducks from travellers at the annual Stow fair, and although both their children attended private schools, they are all fairly scruffy by shopping-mall standards.

They were utterly unimpressed by my venture, because it was all pretty normal for them. Likewise, working-class people I met during the year thought I was a complete tosser. They would comment that it was all right for me to do it out of choice, and could I give them the money I wasn't spending on posh cars and flashy computers?

By the end of the year I think I had finally accepted that I was middle middle class and therefore intrinsically a bit Danish and dull. There was nothing I could do about it. I was never going to be a truly decadent artist living in a run-down Georgian mansion while I scuffed around the ancient floorboards in my father's 50-year-old brogues, which, if I'm honest, is what I have dreamed of being. I am just a middle-class worry mutton who built his own house and has utterly failed to change in the way he dreamed as a young man.

Must go and check how much bog roll we've got.

Greed and Envy

SEPT 28 2007

GREED is the thing we were told we needed in the 1980s. We then felt a little bit bad about it in the 1990s and now it seems we're about to suffer our comeuppance in the noughties.

I always believed that I found greed repugnant, but now as I nod off to sleep, instead of thinking about sex or politics or some breakthrough technology that will produce endless power without damaging the world, I conjure up fictional royalty cheques from the BBC of a staggering size that will arrive in the morning post to solve all our problems. That is tragic and I'm not proud of it.

It was the thesis of the radical Left during my youth that capitalism was fired by greed, that greed was a negative human emotion which always caused harm and that anyone who displayed signs of greed should be publicly shamed.

It turned out that everyone I knew who followed this line of reasoning led a miserable and bitter existence and felt envy every time they came into contact with someone who had new shoes on or who expressed a desire to own their own house. Particular venom was saved for people who seemed happy, because that was a sure sign they were either mentally deluded or selfish capitalists.

Committed members of the political Left, in my casual observation, generally had a crap time. This may have had something to do with the fact that all the radical Left ever did was fall out with each other in more and more complex ways, splitting into ever smaller, ever more exclusive micro-groupings until they disappeared in a puff of old roll-up smoke. Meanwhile, people who decided to use greed as a positive motivating force shot to prominence and power and took over the whole set-up.

For many years the very notion of questioning greed as the driving force behind the economy has been seen not as a threat, but as being slightly daft. The sort of thing vicars and Buddhist hippies drone on about.

Greed is built into the fabric of the society we live in. It's not a word people use in normal conversation, say, when they are discussing the value of their house. You might tell a kid who is stuffing sweets into his mouth and refusing to share them he's a 'greedy guts' but that's about it.

I understand the word 'greed' to mean the desire to take possession of more than you actually need, so I am therefore greedy. I don't need three cars, two houses, six phones, three televisions, nine computers, etc. etc. I thought it was eight computers, but my wife found an old one in her office over the weekend. Ho-hum.

Is that greedy? I know we could live in a caravan with no

telly, no computers and a bucket in a tent to use as a loo – in fact that really appeals to me – but mainly for the sake of my kids, I hope that isn't going to happen. But if I *am* greedy I don't feel I stand out that much. Most of the people around me, the people I queue with on the M40 on the way into London, are just as, if not more, greedy. I have always had the desire to have less, not more, with some very glaring exceptions.

Is it, then, that I stopped buying stuff because I felt greedy? I think it is one of the motivating factors, and even if I am not the greediest individual on the planet, I live in a country that has expressed extreme levels of greed in its long and brutal history, so I am guilty by default.

Envy, on the other hand, is a far more negative emotion and one that was not studied or criticized by the old hard Left. In fact I believe envy was unconsciously encouraged.

'It's all right for you' is an accusation I have heard so many times when discussing wealth, privilege and social mobility among mixed groups of Lefties. I think they were saying 'It is all right for you' because I came from a relatively stable home and neither of my parents fiddled about with my privates, or I grew up in a relatively secure and affluent neighbourhood and country and therefore do not understand the true meaning of deprivation.

'It's all right for you to give up buying new things for a year. You don't need new things because you've already got loads.' There's no real comeback to that – it is all true. So what do I do? Say, 'Stuff you', buy a Porsche Cayenne, drive past a poor person in the rain and make sure I splash them? Surely not.

But even if I can justify my actions to myself, this next 'It's all right for you' is a no-hoper.

When 'It's all right for you, you are a man' is said by a woman, it's the ultimate criticism and there is no comeback. I've tried, 'Yeah, and it's all right for you, you are a white middle-class woman with a university education and wealthy parents,' but they don't rise to the bait. They know they've got me.

I know why it is all right for me. In the global hierarchy of privilege, it is very hard not to see that, certainly for the last thousand years, white men have been in the dominant position. We've got the guns, the money, the physical strength, the political power and the carefully constructed system of the family and hereditary property rights pretty much in the bag. OK, over the last 40 years some of the ladies have been getting a bit stroppy and demanding all sorts of rights and equality; it's been most tiresome. But if you check who's in power and what they're doing with it, the white boys are still running the show.

So maybe it is all right for me, but then are not the people who say these things and have these attitudes prolonging and supporting the very system they have set out to criticize? Perhaps my answer to their accusation should be, 'Of course it's all right for me. I'm a white bloke and I was born to rule. Now wear something tight and make me a coffee, there's a pet.'

It's tempting and Clarksonian in its simplicity. I was born a white male in western Europe in the middle of the 20th century. I am therefore, by definition, privileged. What do I do about it? Abuse that position and make sure everyone who isn't white and male has a bad time as a result of my actions or while in my company? My answer would clearly be no. Should I walk around and moan and envy other white men who have more money or bigger cars or are more famous than me? Well, obviously not, but it's staggering how many white men do that.

I am not above it by any means. I've had to deal with my envious feelings just like anyone else, and the more successful you become, the more aware you are of people who seem ever more successful than you.

I was in the middle of recording a series of *Red Dwarf* many years ago, staying in the house of the wonderful Maria McErlane. I was working in Shepperton Studios, which, just to explain, is about 98 miles from my house and about 15 from Maria's. One evening we were nattering away when I should have been learning lines and Maria, who is incredibly well connected, told me how much Caroline Quentin was earning appearing in *Men Behaving Badly*, and how much Paul Merton got paid for doing *Have I Got News for You*.

I ranted on about how badly I was paid, how I was more or less doing 'charity work' for the blasted BBC, how grossly unfair it all was, how I had a mind to just not turn up the next day and then see if they finally understood what I was worth. Maria, who for all her charming ditzy manner and high-end pals is a woman with her feet firmly on the ground, asked me to listen to myself. I had a job, I was healthy, I was being paid very well for what I was doing. There were thousands of actors waiting tables that very evening, millions more who had given up the hope of ever getting even a walk-on part in a soap, and here I was, whining on like a downtrodden refugee.

Not only did she make me feel a bit of a prat for having an envy attack, she also relieved me of the burden of it. It doesn't matter if someone is richer or slimmer or more famous than you, because no matter how lucky or unlucky you are, there is always someone more or less lucky than you, who envies you and thinks you are lazy and overprivileged. Once you shed the burden of envy, life is far more relaxing.

Greed, however, is a harder thing to be rid of.

I went into a busy London newsagent's the other day to buy a paper. This was after my making-do year, so is still a newish experience for me and I relish it. This time when I didn't buy anything it was for a completely different reason. I just couldn't wait long enough to get to the man behind the cash till and pay. It was a Friday evening and the place was jammed with people buying lottery tickets. They were buying them in the hope of winning millions of pounds, the greedy hope that they would suddenly, with virtually no effort, have more money than they could ever possibly need.

I have never entered the National Lottery thing. I wouldn't even know how to do it, but I want to point out this is not because 'It's all right for you, you don't need to enter the lottery cos you're so rich already.' I'm not rich but, far more importantly, I think it's a stupid thing to do. I heard an interesting statistic about the lottery on the radio: you are more likely to pick up a winning lottery ticket that someone has dropped on the street than you are to buy a winning one.

I couldn't live with myself if I bought a lottery ticket and nurtured the greedy hope that I might suddenly become a multi-millionaire. I'd feel like such an idiot. I'm rubbish at maths, but I know that the chances of matching all six numbers (I didn't know there were six numbers until I looked it up) is one in 14 million. It could be you, yes of course; and it could be me who becomes the first non-native radical anarchist president of the United States and flies around the White House on a hover board.

Of all the human vices, gambling is the one that truly mystifies me, but surely it is powered by a kind of greed. I just don't get it and, as I waited in frustration to pay for my paper, I felt like shouting, 'For pity's sake, let's riot on the street and demand that the wealth of the nation is distributed evenly throughout society. We've got more chance of getting a few quid that way.' Needless to say I put the newspaper back on the pile, said nothing and left the shop.

I spent three days in Las Vegas a few years ago and never put one coin in one slot machine or threw one dice or turned over one card. I still loved it, it's the maddest place I've ever seen, but I just don't need to gamble.

My mother once explained to me that I didn't need to because of my profession, which is a gamble every day. When I told her stories of the vagaries of the business we call show, she was always horrified by the dangers and the chronic insecurity it engenders. She was right. I never know where the next job is coming from, if anyone will like anything I've written, if the series I'm in will get another commission. All I do is gamble from dawn till dusk, every day. No wonder I don't want to do it as a hobby. But greed does have a lot to do with it too, and that is something I have never felt comfortable with.

Again, this must go back to parenting. For all the multiple failings I have achieved in that field, I don't think my kids are that greedy. Both Judy and I have hammered on since day one about sharing and not being greedy. There is something uniquely unsettling about seeing your kid sitting down and munching a bag of crisps while their best friend sits next to them with nothing.

'Share your crisps, darling,' you hiss with a fake smile. 'Don't be a greedy gubbins.' You then watch in mild horror as your little angel begrudgingly fishes out a carefully chosen crispette from the bag and hands it to the poor mite next to her. Oh, the joy they bring.

But what I really can't stand in the greed arena is when other people make a lot of money out of something you do. This goes from the woman who squirts the jam into doughnuts in the factory and the man who tightens the wheel nuts on the car production line to the TV actor who is tricked out of royalty payments for video sales by some flaky agreement between his 'union' and the association of producers. As you may have guessed from the last sentence, there is a certain amount of personal history there. It was a long time ago and I am over it now.

If your job is actually creating something that someone else sells and they make far more money than you do out of that sale, is it greedy to want a slightly bigger fraction of the money that is being made? It probably is greedy, but it's based on fairly sound moral principles.

Maybe greed is good as long as it comes from the bottom up, but of course when that does happen the full might of the system is turned against that poor person.

That said, as a general rule, the less you feel greed and envy, the happier you will be. Sadly, you will also be poorer and surrounded by very wealthy people who don't have to work hard and who are content to spend the money which, in a fairer world, would belong to you.

THE ACTUAL need for any consumer item is, if you think about it carefully, very small. We don't truly need about 80 per cent of the stuff we have, but why shouldn't we have it? We have managed to convince ourselves we 'need' absurdly expensive things.

What we really need are the three basics: food, clothing and shelter. We always have and always will. At the time of writing we spend very little on food, loads on clothes and saddle ourselves with crippling debt for shelter. The rest we spend on stuff we clearly don't need in any true physical way, it just fills the void at the centre of the human soul. Or is that just me?

My year of making do allowed me to consider this question for the first time in many years. Is there a better way to live in the present day, in the present social and political climate, and if so, how on earth do we change?

Need

One of the reasons I keep going back to my early years is because, like so many people, I started out with such good intentions, only to see them ruined by the rain of life until they lay in a soggy grey pile of embarrassment at my feet.

I managed to avoid what used to quaintly be called 'the rat race' for a surprisingly long time during my early adulthood. I worked but I didn't have a job. I lived in houses but I didn't own them or pay rent because I was a squatter. When I didn't live in squats I lived in the back of a converted furniture truck, not for weekend breaks or the summer holidays, but for two years solid.

Living in the truck changed my life very dramatically.

Up until that point I suffered very severe insecurity. It wasn't some vague notion of inner anxiety; it was based on very real experience. The problem with squatting was you were living on the very edge of the law. It's hard to explain to anyone who hasn't done it. Squatting was sort of legal, but you could be thrown out of the house you were living in at any time. This meant you didn't know where you were going to be living from one day to the next. You could never 'get it together', as I was so fond of trying to do at the time.

I had nothing to fall back on except my parents, and thankfully I always knew I could go back to them and have a bath and wash my clothes and eat reassuringly plain if slightly overcooked food.

But living in the truck was a total change, because for the first time in my life I had one place I could really call my own, and it didn't have the dead weight of responsibility like a mortgage would have done. I lived in it with my girlfriend,

Lee, and a scruffy mutt of a dog called Ruffage. It was true we had to keep moving, but at least the house came with us when we did so.

The other thing that living in such a confined space taught me was how important it was to be tidy, to put things away, and also not to have too much stuff. We really did have only what we needed. We couldn't carry anything else – we didn't have a loft to store unwanted things in or a spare room to pile full of boxes. We truly did have only what we directly needed, and that pleased me.

I must point out that we were very bourgeois hippie travellers. We always asked permission to park up and, because of our connections, we stayed in the most amazing places. We never left any mess; in fact I would say we were fastidious about the state of our 'hatchin tan'. That was an old travellers' term meaning campsite we learned from some proper old-school travellers we met outside Warminster in 1976.

There is no doubt that this was a wonderful period of my life and of course living in the truck during 1976 was a huge blessing, as this was the hottest summer in recorded history. It was a lovely time to be young, footloose and living outdoors. Well, we slept in the truck, but we parked in some wonderful places, like an orchard in Suffolk or, at one point, on a clifftop overlooking the sea near Plymouth. It was absurdly idyllic.

From that moment on I have always wanted less and for many years I managed to succeed in this goal. I was constantly penniless and didn't seem to have the ability to acquire more. However, due to my social-chameleon qualities, I would occasionally get in with rich folk. I'd see the inside of their houses, sit at their dinner tables and amuse them for my supper. It was at these moments, usually when 'popping to the loo', that I would take in the wealth and comfort of these places and wonder what it would be like to have so much.

When I met my wife, Judy (there we go, I said 'my wife'), in August 1988, I had a futon bed, three chairs and a homemade desk. Judy had one big bag full of clothes and a portable typewriter. We were both stand-up comics, Judy far more successful than me and much better at it. I don't say that out of any false modesty, it was simply true, plus she'd performed as a comic far more than me and she'd won prizes in Australia, one of which was a ticket to the UK and a slot at the Edinburgh Festival, which is where we met.

Starting from this very low point, and remembering that we weren't students when we met – Judy was in her late twenties and I was over thirty – we had gone a long way in adult life and picked up very little baggage on the journey.

In 1992 Judy went for a drive in the country with one of her Aussie pals while I was working in Los Angeles. During that drive she found a house for sale in a little village and went into a local estate agent in Stow-on-the-Wold to enquire about it. We had discussed buying somewhere to live, but although we were both working we didn't have a massive amount of money. Buying somewhere in London seemed impossible. We knew we could keep Judy's rented flat and the dream was to buy somewhere cheap in Dorset or Herefordshire.

On my return to England two weeks later we went to look at this house, but we never found it. Neither of us knew the area and although some names rang a bell from my childhood it wasn't somewhere I was familiar with. We went into the estate agent's in Stow-on-the-Wold and the lady started showing us properties for sale in the local area. She flicked through pages in a large book – everything she showed us was either comically expensive or really ugly, quite often both, but one page she turned past quickly, saying, 'You won't want that. It's wooden.'

And 16 years later, that's where we still live, in a wooden house in an ancient Cotswold village, utterly incongruous and out of place but somehow entirely appropriate. Not only that, but in those 16 years we have built up a healthy pile of stuff. I am being cruel here, because it's not stuff we don't need. I mean, a sofa, while not being an essential, is very nice to flop on of an evening. No one needs bookshelves, but they are very useful. We don't need a kitchen table, but life is much harder without one.

However, all these things weigh me down. This isn't a burden that I share with Judy, as it clearly doesn't worry her in the least. When times are bad in the life of our fractious, tempestuous and passionate family, I fantasize about a small wooden hut in the woods. I don't have one, but it's where I dream of hiding when I am not coping with the demands of fatherhood in a mature and creative way.

In my little dream shed I would need some dented aluminium cooking utensils, a wood-burning stove, a cot to sleep in, a dog basket for my old smelly dog, a small box of tools and some candles. That would be it. I would have straggly long hair and a beard down to my wide leather belt, all my clothes would be brown and no doubt I would stink to high heaven.

The dream is 'that is all I need'. Obviously it's absurd and unrealistic. I have two children to look after; I can't go and hide in the woods, ignoring them, but that's not to say the thought doesn't occasionally arise.

I would of course love it if my kids needed less. Nothing in life happens overnight, but with the passing of time, as they have grown and developed, they start to 'need' more. When they were giggling little toddlers they didn't need anything other than food, shelter, clothes, love and the patience of their parents. They also needed their friends, a story read to them, some paper and crayons to do drawings with – we always did a lot of that – some mud and sticks, some old pots to make mixtures in, a dog to go for walks with, sometimes with their dad. Now they are that much older, it appears they need a great deal more. I still want to read stories to them, but they prefer to listen to music or audio books on their iPods. I still want to do a puppet show for them – that has been officially classified as 'so tragic and so gay!'

I understand they're right. I want them to go out and play, and they do. In my son's case, on skateboards – he has got through literally dozens and their shattered remains are mounted like trophies on the wall of his room. My daughter goes out and plays on a pony. She has one at the local livery yard and he's marvellous and popular enough to have his pictures all over her room. Skateboards and ponies are a lot more responsibility for me than a pot full of mud in the garden and I cannot say my children need them. I have seen the obvious benefits they receive from having them. My son's skateboard tricks are on his YouTube channel and he's learned fairly advanced video-editing from creating them.

My daughter's confidence and independence have been increased to a very marked extent by her involvement with her pony.

As for me, I clearly don't need a 24-inch screen to write this book on, I could write it on a bit of old paper with a pencil, so what am I moaning about?

I think my big concern is the trouble people find themselves in when they no longer have what they are used to having. I'm pretty sure I could adjust fairly well to a sudden downturn, but I'm worried my children would find it much tougher. They have been born into such a privileged home in such a privileged era, and I constantly experience the classic parental frustration when they don't seem to understand this fact. How dumb am I? I must be such a bore for them, because I am constantly saying, 'You should be grateful ... You are so lucky ... There are so many children who don't have the opportunities you do ... You don't seem to appreciate what your mother and I have done for you.'

The only response they can make, and they usually do, is, 'Get over it, Dad.' Oh, the joy they bring.

I have realized that not shopping for a year was very much born out of the desire to not need so much. In fact I want to achieve a state of mind where I don't truly need anything and don't spend any time thinking about it.

Grace

OCT
23
2007

THE BIRTHDAY of my late mother, someone who appeared, certainly to her friends, to be a woman of grace. I have learned a lot from thinking about my mother since she died. She was in fact a very angry woman and under the gentle state of grace she displayed in public was a seething cauldron of resentment and anger which would occasionally leak out. I'm sure she had every reason to be angry, but, as I am discovering on a daily basis, anger really doesn't help. So my struggle to achieve grace is very much about trying to shed the heavy cloak of anger I have inherited from her and developed myself.

I cannot help feeling that the archetypal human being in the archetypal shopping mall is about as far from a state of grace as it is possible to get. I wish I could be saying this from a lofty position of spiritual oneness, knowingness and wholeness, but I have rarely if ever achieved a state of grace in my life, even for a couple of seconds. The thing is, though, I feel I can recognize it in others, which gives me some solace: at least I know what grace is, even if it forever eludes me. It might seem odd for a rough, tough, semi-reconstructed petrol-head and angry foul-mouthed show-off, but the desire to reach a state of grace has been a constant in my life.

In my casual ruminations on the subject of grace, I have come up with a standard set of undefendable assumptions about those who do seem genuinely gracious. Gracious people, in my vast experience, are mostly women over 40, and very occasionally men over 60. They are not primarily from any one particular social or racial group, but it is safe to say they probably don't spend an enormous amount of time shopping.

I have a friend in America who is a gracious person. She is quiet but very aware of the world around her, gentle but without doubt very strong. Her life has been beset by all the problems many of us have had to face: children, divorce, remarriage, work satisfaction, the loss of a parent in childhood which spun her early life in a radical new direction. Yet through all this she has remained very gracious.

I think I may have been hoping that taking time out from consuming and the all-encompassing experience of removing material desire would allow me to enter a state of grace without much effort. I have to admit that this didn't happen. Somehow life, parenting and work constantly got in the way, diverting me from my imagined true calling. I'm also worried that if I did become really full of grace I'd be really bored. You can't be a graceful person with a short attention span, can you? If you can, I want to be the first to achieve it.

Grace

Last weekend I was in a really good mood, the sun was shining, the sky clear, my family were all in the house and there were no extra children, no sleepovers or pressing transport arrangements to bother about. We had breakfast together and no one had a sulk, row or bad temper flare-up, even me, and that's a good sign. My wife was coping with the stress as she took one child to an extracurricular educational assignation while I was getting ready to take the other child to a leisure-based pony-related activity. It was a normal Saturday morning and all was good; I was smiling and full of grace. I started to walk into our kitchen to get the car keys and, as I grabbed my coat, it is possible I wasn't 100 per cent aware of my immediate surroundings. I didn't notice that one foot was on my son's casually discarded school bag at the foot of the stairs. Why my body weight was angled in such a way as to cause this bag to slip from under me so rapidly is still one of the great mysteries of physics, but slip it did and very suddenly. I landed on my left elbow and hip and the pain really knocked the wind out of me. My daughter screamed 'Dad!' so it must have looked quite alarming too, but knowing what I am like when I experience an accident like this she rapidly backed off. I can now look back at that moment as I hobbled around the house trying to control the thrashing monster of my temper as a supreme test of 'he who wishes to attain grace'. I failed the test with aplomb.

The questions 'Why did he have to leave his bag there?' and 'Can't anyone put anything away in this wretched house?' did cross my mind, but I didn't say them.

This was a complete accident, it could have happened to anyone. What I would like to know is how a graceful person responds when experiencing that sort of sudden upset.

It's not that I want to float around in yellow robes, being given rice by poverty-stricken farmers. I just want to be able to deal with the accidents of life without immediately feeling hard done by or bad-tempered and angry.

It's often been the case that people attempt to become more spiritually whole and therefore more peaceful by withdrawing from the normal society of their era and living a very austere life somewhere remote from the developed world. While that is attractive, it does seem like something of a cop-out.

Monks on an island, Buddhist hippies in a run-down stately home, Scientologists in their weird temple things, yoga fanatics on retreat on a Greek island, they are all 'getting away from it all'. I understand the idea, but what is 'it all'? Surely it's the world each of us has been engaged in building. This world wasn't imposed on us by some weird outside force beyond our control. We made it.

So if you remove all the caustic, electric stimulation of modern life, the idea is you can become one, become spiritually whole again, blah de blah. Well, if the modern world is so wrong, and I don't believe it is, wouldn't it be better to use your energies to do something about it? Would it not be preferable to achieve a state of grace while living within the modern world? Isn't that more of an achievement? I think just about anyone can calm down if they are given the right peaceful environment, but how am I going to pay the rent and get the kids to school on time if I am on a Greek island sitting in a funny position for three weeks?

What did happen, though, when I stopped buying things was that I was faced with the true selfishness of my life. This is also the curse of parenting, because, in the microcosm of the family, I am anything but selfish. I am the living God of self-sacrifice. I am on call pretty much all the time. I am head of IT and technical backup for our family. Someone's computer, phone or car is always up the spout and I am the one who is called to sort it out. I am assistant head of transportation, clocking up hundreds of miles of logistical travel a week ensuring my children have a fully rounded social life.

However, as soon as I walk out of the front door, I am selfishness personified. Although I give paltry sums to charities I support, it barely covers my feelings of guilt, let alone actually helps the charities. I began to wonder if I actually donated some of my time every week to helping a local charity the payback would be a momentary state of grace. I am planning to do this, but I don't think I can do it with such a consciously selfish motive in the background. Surely a truly gracious person would do charity work and barely notice, because they wouldn't have their eye on the main chance like I always seem to.

So, although I say my mother was an angry woman, she clearly did seem graceful to so many people. The gathering at her funeral was immense; she was obviously adored by everyone who met her. To say she was angry gives the wrong impression. She was kind, she had time for other people and she did endless, tireless charity work. She spent years delivering meals on wheels and didn't live long enough to receive them, she worked for the Red Cross and Mencap, she made sure all our early theatrical presentations gathered money for the NSPCC. It was just that every now and then the anger would come through and I would witness her spit and rail against some, to me, quite petty injustice. Of course, my mother was an avid *Daily Mail* reader and that particular publication doesn't help anyone's equilibrium. They never have a free-offer banner on their cover proclaiming, 'Read our new guide to being gracious and forgiving, page 10'. It's not going to happen, is it? It's always, 'Now they want us to pay for immigrant mothers to fly first class to Disneyland!'

My mother constantly sent me clippings from the *Daily Mail* she thought I would be interested in. I have to say I wasn't. For a short period I sent her clippings from *Black Dwarf*, an anarchist publication of the 1970s which espoused violent revolution, or from *Marxism Today*, a trendy lefty rag of the 1980s, but they didn't have much impact. Now I don't get anything from her and I do miss it, and when I get angry over some trifling concern, I am reminded of her, so I suppose that's comforting.

IS THE fact that we drive cars, fly in planes and keep our TVs on standby really making the world warmer? I know this question is heresy and I'm not asking it because I'm secretly funded by an oil company and want to undermine the good work of the thousands of dedicated scientists and activists who have struggled long and hard to get the global population to at least start to see the error of their ways. But is it?

The one simple fact that made me stop and think as I drove along in my low-output vehicle, on the way to the recycling bins, was news of the discovery of a Norse settlement on the coast of Greenland dating back maybe a thousand years. They practised farming, raised cattle and built houses in Greenland. Which can only mean one thing: it was warmer then than it is now, which also means that the world has got colder and warmer before Carl Benz turned over the first internal combustion engine about 120 years ago. Before some dude in a tall hat fired up the first boiler that powered a steam engine that drove a spinning jenny in Lancashire and started to fill the air with smog.

It is also important to remember that the big fear in the good old, oft-referred-to 1970s was global freezing, the coming ice age. From 1945 until about 1975, global temperatures fell, which also makes you stop and think, because without doubt this was a period of fantastic economic and industrial growth around the world.

I lived through the winter of 1963 and, believe me, it was pretty nippy. We couldn't go to school for a week simply because we couldn't get there. Even my dad couldn't get to work, and he would happily have waded waist-deep through human effluent to get to work, anything to get away from his blasted family for the day.

I also lived through the summer of 1976, which was fantastic, very hot and dry from April until late September. For those too young to remember it, there was not a drop of rain for that whole five-month period, crystal-clear skies week after week, amazing temperatures, not a blade of green grass in the country. Buildings started to crack because the ground dried so much it shrank. I had a really deep suntan and I never left the south of England. I have yet to experience another summer like it in this country and that was over 30 years ago. I also recall only a couple of years back there was endless news about the terrible drought in the south-east of England. Hosepipe bans, no car washing, no garden watering, massive sales spike for water butts – it was catastrophic, with all the reports classifying the situation as terminal. People were literally going to die of thirst, according to the newspapers, radio and TV bulletins. Now it's floods: the water table is so high, water is leaking out of the ground. It's all a disaster; it's all much worse than it has ever been. I suppose. Except from where I'm standing it's mainly much better than it was.

Here's a clue. Try tuning in to the positive-news channel. You know, the one reporting all the positive stories in which people come up with actual solutions to problems and suggest ways of dealing with the challenges facing us. Never seen it? We all know it doesn't exist and, even if it did, no one would watch it. News is, by definition, bad news. That's what makes us talk to each other; that's what we like to talk about.

But carbon is different, because there are some things we can do, immediately and personally, to change the amount we release into the atmosphere, and there are some things we simply can't. I was filming at a container port at the end of my making-do year and it seemed very appropriate. All day I watched giant ships enter Southampton Harbour, unload about 1,000 containers, load up another 800 or so and sail away before the tide went out. Frenetic doesn't describe it, the tonnage and scale are too big for one person to see. The container ship that arrived when we were there is powered by steam turbines, the engine itself roughly the size of two substantial family homes. It uses about 200 tons of fuel a day when it is sailing across the sea, pumping out quite mind-boggling amounts of CO_2 every day of the year. These things aren't kept in a garage or parked on a street at night, they are running non-stop. All for us, so we can buy an iPod or a six-pack of socks for £1.99 from TK Maxx.

Then of course there are planes, and this one, no matter where you stand on the issue, is a no-brainer. If you buy a packet of ready-trimmed beans at your local supermarket that were grown in Kenya, they have been flown here on a Boeing 747 freight plane. It does 18 gallons to the mile and leaves its harmful gasses where they really pack a punch, 38,000 feet up. I buy these beans, I'm not innocent, but I certainly don't buy them as often as I did. We have to find another way to eat beans. Here's a suggestion: buy ones that were grown here and wait until they are available seasonally. No, it's not going to work, is it? Not until those Kenyan beans are £30 a packet.

My problem with the fashionable portrayal of carbon footprints and global warming is that it's almost presented as a joke. It's what do-gooder liberals are supposedly foisting on us and making our Range Rover-driving experience more miserable. I don't deny that these events are taking place, but I simply don't trust the system that informs us about them. We should constantly question every *fait accompli* that we are presented with. That is, I believe, our duty as citizens. As they used to say in the 1970s, 'Don't believe the man.'

Misogyny

THIS MAY seem an odd chapter title, but what I am attempting to do is frame a critique of how I see contemporary women without falling into the old traps. Either the old duffer in the gentlemen's club, idly speculating about the opposite sex with little or no understanding, or the bully boy in the pub who's looking at the picture of a topless page-three model and leering at her while proudly declaring she must be 'a slag'.

Women have fascinated me my entire life. I feel very comfortable in their company and love their way of looking at things. Most of the time. This aside, I have been unable to ignore a certain aspect of their behaviour which leaves me, and clearly many other heterosexual men, baffled: the need to 'shop'.

It is possible that I am more aware of this desire than men of other generations because my peer group of women, the

225

well-educated, emancipated, challenging women who came of age in the 1970s, expressed deep and well-argued criticisms of women's need to shop, to decorate themselves for the pleasure and delectation of men. I was with them all the way. Go for it, sisters. Don't waste your money on such frippery. Let the men deal with it, because it's their problem.

Then the years passed and I started to notice something. I struggled against it, I designated the thought misogynist, it was part of my sexist view of the world, it was typical of a man to judge women in that way. I fought off this observation with every ounce of my inner new man.

I failed.

I worried that these opinions were part of the endless power struggle between men and women that has been and remains my obsession, and a damaging one to boot. However, this worrying view I now have of women will not go away.

Women love shopping. Not all women, but, let's face it, a very large proportion. The often referred to 'high street' is dedicated to her pleasure; it is a foreign and strange place for a man. So I have been wondering why this is the case. What is it about buying clothes that gives women so much pleasure and fulfilment?

The very obvious answer that most men take for granted is that women want to look nice, and the subtext of that is that they want to look nice for us.

Wrong, and here's a good example.

A young woman I knew socially, I shall call her M, was very generously gifted in both intellect and looks, sharp as a razor, observant, successful and delightful company. We never dated or anything like it, but we did go to the movies together one memorable night. Now, the reason M stays in my mind is because of the profound lack of sexual tension between us. I accept that men are thick when it comes to women and relationships, I have plenty of experiences to reinforce that view, but I'm not that dumb. I knew M didn't fancy me, and I also knew she knew I didn't fancy her. We had a lot of friends in common and I liked her company. So I turned up at her rather luxurious apartment (it belonged to Daddy) one evening to find that she had been painting the spare room. She was wearing paint-spattered old jeans and a washed-out T-shirt. For the first time since I had known her she looked scruffy and relaxed. M was very conscious of her appearance; I found her company a little tense for this reason, because I knew I could never keep up with her sartorial standards. I was a scruff, a boho, a lazy unshaven bloke who's only plus was that I was a little obsessed with personal hygiene. I may have looked grubby but I was obsessively, almost gayly clean.

Seeing M in this dishevelled and relaxed state wasn't something I was prepared for. I suddenly found her rather attractive for the first time. I needn't have worried. In fact while I waited for her to 'get ready' I started to relax. The fact that I was waiting for her to get ready could only mean one thing. She was transforming herself from this rather attractive, relaxed woman into the 1980s power-dresser that I had known and feared.

Sure enough, 15 minutes later she appeared, hair creatively styled, make-up heavily applied, clothes immaculately fashionable. I breathed a sigh of relief. I didn't find her in the least bit attractive any more. We went to the movies, had a coffee afterwards and talked about films and the film industry (in which she worked) and I dropped her back home with no more than a peck on the cheek.

It was that night I realized something I have always wanted to relate to young men I know and work with. Women don't get dressed up to attract you, matey boy, they get dressed up for each other. Maybe other men worked this out much younger than I did. Maybe it shows I am more vain, because I assumed that women dressed up to attract men or, more specifically, me. It is important for a man to understand that, at a fundamental level, women view us at best as a necessary accoutrement and ingredient in procreation, but generally as a bit of an encumbrance, and in the worst cases an annoyance or downright danger.

Women use make-up and clothes to impress other women. I am ashamed at how long it took me to realize that. The vast majority of men, when asked, will not generally know if a woman is or isn't wearing make-up, they will have little or no opinion about her clothes, or where they come from, how much they cost or if they are or are not in fashion.

The vast majority of men prefer a woman who has not had her breasts augmented with silicone. Women don't make their breasts bigger to attract men. They do it to impress and raise their status with other women. Women don't want to remain slim and young-looking to attract a man. They want to remain like that because of the visual and emotional impact it has on other women.

I firmly believe, for sound biological reasons, women are far more competitive with each other than men are with each other, and very often a man's role in a woman's life is part of that competition. A woman will love and struggle to maintain a relationship with an attractive, successful male after they have conceived children in order to use him as a symbol, a sign for other women. In very crude terms, a successful woman is saying to other women, look at me, I've got a narrower waist, bigger breasts, more attractive and intelligent children, a newer frock, more make-up and cooler hair than you, and I've got this man who is taller and richer than your husband.

I can't help being sad about this understanding. I don't want it to be true but it is reinforced every time I go into a shopping mall or department store. Capitalism recognizes this need and exploits it with ruthless efficiency. There is no point in a man telling a woman, 'I don't care if you don't dress well or wear loads of make-up, I love you for who you are.' This is not only a waste of breath but, more importantly and worse, tantamount to an attack on her dignity and inner well-being. As a man you are trying, no matter how benign your intentions, to undermine her status with other women and that is destined to be a disastrous course of action.

On reflection I think my confusion in this area has to stem from the generation of women with whom I came of age. My generation of middle-class, educated women – the Harriet Harman generation – seems to have moved from the glorious feminist revolution, where all things designed to make women conform to a narrow sexual stereotype were rejected, to the enthusiastic adoption of über-consumerism and the obsessive observation of fashion and trend.

I feel a bit of a fool, because I somehow didn't notice the change.

The proud ability to shop, the endless desire to shop, the casual adoption of the many supposedly humorous excuses for needless consumerism have been picked up and run with by my generation of women. Obviously they have been influenced by the generations of women who have come after them who truly did seem to be 'born to shop'.

I am not sure if this behaviour has been cleverly introduced by the people who run shops, and a lot of them are women, or by the female shoppers themselves. These female shoppers are supported at every turn by the world around them, by the rows of glossy women's magazines I have seen on the newsagents' shelves but never actually read. And by the mainstream TV industry, particularly the commercial sector, which editorially is now dominated by women and makes programmes for women, many of which, quite apart from the adverts, are dedicated to encouraging women to consume in some way or another.

Of course, all the time I think about this I can come up with dozens of women I have met who have sidestepped the whole charade, who are stylish and beautiful and who spend little or no money on pointless consumerism, who don't buy new clothes every week and who could no more go into a shopping mall and feel good about it than I could.

That said, watch TV on a weekday evening and you will see mainly women on the screen being told they are too fat, badly dressed or utterly without style. They will be told this by other women or in the more imaginative cases by an amusing homosexual man. There will be no reference in these shows to men in general. They do not enter the picture, because, lads, it's not about us.

Or go to a shopping mall on a Saturday morning and you will see mostly women strolling across the marble-effect floors, festooned with those large paper bags proudly bearing the label of some 'designer'.

OK, yes, go to a big computer store on the outside of town and you will see crowds of slightly nerdy men fingering bubble packs of obscure cables or slavering over high-capacity flash memory sticks, but I would argue that there are more women's clothing stores than out-of-town computer showrooms.

I started observing women and shopping at a very early age. I think I would have been about eight years old and it's a memory that is forever burned into me. I was staying at my grandmother's house in Cheltenham and one day she and my wonderful Auntie Peggy took me shopping to the Bon Marché in Gloucester. I remember the name of this store so vividly, but I'm sure it no longer exists (it was probably a precursor to John Lewis or something). I have just looked it up and it is now a Debenhams, but the Bon Marché dated from the 1930s and I can now inform you that it hadn't changed one bit when I went there in the 1960s. I don't remember going there or coming back, though the journey would undoubtedly have been by bus, but I do remember being there, waiting for hours as Grandma and Auntie Peggy happily discussed the colour of a hat or the cut of a coat.

Auntie Peggy, my mother's older sister, was and still is a very stylish woman, very unlike my mother, who, let's be kind, had a unique style of her own that, thankfully, I never saw replicated anywhere else.

Grandma and Auntie Peggy spent what seemed to me like days looking at shoes and gloves, and every now and then they asked me if I was all right. I was a very polite little boy with a short-back-and-sides haircut, ironed shorts and brown leather T-bar sandals. My brother's old ones, well worn and no doubt too big for me. I would tell them I was fine and later they would buy me an iced bun in the department store tearoom. What has stayed with me, though, is that they didn't actually buy anything, they just looked and tried things on. I must have related this shopping excursion to my parents at some point, because for many years afterwards, if I kicked off about going to some stately home or castle on one of my mother's endless educational trips, I would be reminded that I could go to the Bon Marché with Grandma instead, which made even the dullest stately home a positive theme park of childish enjoyment by comparison.

This experience has come back to me regularly when I have accompanied various girlfriends or my wife on shopping trips. That doesn't sound right. I'm not accompanying either various girlfriends or my wife now. I mean in the dim and distant, before I met my wife, I went shopping with various girlfriends. Phew, cleared that up.

Anyway, it's almost a physically painful experience and I am clearly not the only man who suffers from this. During these rare excursions I do get a certain perverse enjoyment from seeing other uncomfortable men carrying armloads of shopping bags through town centres on Saturday afternoons. They will be waiting outside changing rooms, knowing they are almost certainly doomed to say the wrong thing when their partner emerges wearing some peculiar new top or a frock that might suit an emaciated 15-year-old catwalk model but makes them look a bit tubby.

That's the trouble I have. Maybe I am gay, because I do have an eye for such things. When a woman wears the wrong thing, I do notice. If they are wearing the right thing, I don't think I notice anything.

Judy is anything but a fashion victim. When I met her she possessed one bag of clothes, which were all second-hand. They were all very worn and most of them were costumes. Before her stand-up career she was a circus performer and stomped on stage or into the circus ring to do a miraculous egg-balancing act she had learned in China. She wore, if memory serves, a black tutu and big black boots and she shouted angrily at the audience. Breakfast at home now, 25 years later, isn't that much different. The audience loved it. I loved it. And very rapidly I loved her. I went to see her again and again and had to wait a year before we met properly. It's a romantic story and has nothing to do with consumerism in any way so I won't go on.

However, she is a good example. In those days it would have been easy to store all her clothes in a carrier bag. Now we really need to build another extension. I'm exaggerating for cheap comic effect and I will pay for it, but from a man's point of view she does have a lot of outfits. If I look through her built-in hanging cupboard thing, her wardrobe, whatever it is called, there are items lovingly hung there I swear I have never seen her wear. She is like me in many ways in that she generally wears the same old worn-out thing when we are both working at home.

As I have said, we men assume in our egotistical way that women dress up to make themselves attractive to us. This is arrogant nonsense. They don't give a flying poop what we think. After the age of about 17 a woman only dresses to either impress or protect herself from the gaze of other women. Men don't really notice unless they can see through the clothes, and if they do notice and have an opinion, then, let's face it, and without meaning to be derogatory, they are gay. Which is a good thing. If it wasn't for the wonderful influence of gay men, the average heterosexual male would look even worse today than he does.

Actually, while I'm being a bit gay, let me say something about football shirts. I can't hold it in any longer. In the last thousand years the most ugly thing anyone has come up with for a man to wear off the football field is a football shirt. They just look so rubbish. A short fat man in a football shirt is the very worst look it is possible to imagine. Football shirts make shell suits look cool. They make a man in medieval clothes buying petrol for his old Land Rover look cool. Good, better now ... Back to women and misogyny.

It's the same with make-up: I never have any idea if a woman is wearing make-up, I can't tell. Other women can tell, because they notice everything. Patient and understanding women have suggested that I can tell when a woman is wearing too much make-up, and this is true, too much make-up is really scary for a man. Does she think we don't know she's covered in a pound and a half of vaguely flesh-coloured Sandtex? What does she look like without it? It makes men worry.

Quick shocking fact and easily Google-able, someone (probably a journalist, so pinch of salt on standby) has worked out that the average woman in the UK spends £8,500 on make-up in her lifetime.

When I was thinking about this whole area of mystery I walked through the make-up department of Selfridges store on London's Oxford Street. I had been there before, but I had never really looked, as I usually keep my head down and hope no heavily made-up young woman will try to spray me with some pungent scent. This time I wanted to take it all in. The store and the cosmetic companies were clearly going to a colossal effort, but the products were 90 per cent packaging and surely the women behind the counters were a very bad advert for the range. They all seemed to be made up to an almost comic extent. This time I truly did notice they were wearing make-up, even without my glasses on. There is serious money in this business and the effort, knowledge and care that women lavish on themselves is, finally, beyond comprehension or judgement from a man. It became more and more obvious as I wandered about, looking at the wonderfully presented arrays of lipsticks, weird ointments and creams, that this industry has nothing to do with mating, breeding, seducing or any other activity that related to men.

The mystery, which is in some ways defined by the term 'fashion', is that it appears to a casually observing male that women all want to look the same. I spend most of my time seeing other men my age and wanting to do anything I can possibly do not to look like them.

Of course, most men my age wear suits when they are at work and I have never been big on suits. It seems so unfair that women get to wear skirts, dresses or trousers in a huge range of styles and colours, while men wear suits which are either grey or another shade of slightly duller grey.

The fashion industry is a huge mystery to me. It is something I am barely aware of and in some ways I would love to go to a proper fashion show just to see what it is really like. Do the not so thin middle-aged women who watch the thin teenage girls walking along the catwalk in that peculiar stomping heavy-footed way they all have genuinely imagine themselves in the same clothes? Do they? That was a question. What can they possibly imagine when they see an emaciated, barely pubescent girl wearing something fabulous? That if they wore the same thing they would look like that? I don't understand, and no woman has been able to explain.

'It makes me feel better if I wear something nice.'

No, I am simply never going to understand, and although after my year of not shopping I am itching to say to women in general, 'Stop buying this rubbish. You don't need it and you will still be able to breed without it, as men will find you attractive if you are wearing rags or a 90-year-old coat.' There is no point saying anything and all this chapter has done is highlight my misogyny. That's 30 years of reconstruction and behaviour modification down the pan, what a shame.

A wonderful event happened while I was in the middle of writing this chapter. I was having a pub lunch after a long Cotswold walk with an old friend of the family. While there she told me she has been invited to a very posh event, entry to the Royal Enclosure at some horse race in a couple of months' time, and she said, I quote, 'I have absolutely nothing to wear.'

I was anxious. I know how she feels. If I had to go somewhere posh and I only had my patched old trousers and worn-out shoes, I would feel really out of place. However, this statement didn't give the true picture, as she then went on to list a possible outfit that sounded very smart to me. Lots of names of designers and descriptions of skirts and coats, boots and tops. I assumed this was what she had seen in a shop and what she had decided to buy for this special day. But no, you've guessed it, this was the list of things she already had. Absolutely nothing to wear doesn't mean what men think it means; rather, it means, 'I have tons of clothes I already don't wear, and I really need to buy more to make me feel good enough to attend a horse race in the Royal Enclosure. However, it is highly likely when I go that I won't wear any of the clothes I have bought and will instead revert to the original list.'

I realize now that although I have often mentioned the 50-plus years of experience, it doesn't make a jot of difference in this case. I will never understand. I just have to live with it and not comment, not judge, smile and maybe very discreetly wonder.

Hope

NOV
21
2007

NOT AN easy month to remain optimistic, November: no hope, no future, no joy. There's some sort of slightly naff poem I've heard on Radio 4's *Poetry Please* a few years ago which goes something like that.

There are certainly days in November when I find it hard not to ask myself if there is any hope. Early in the morning I wander around the hills and fields near where I live, trying to absorb hope from nature. I look up into the magnificent clear blue sky (I'm describing fairly rare weather during my morning walk here) and breathe deeply – ahh, the timeless beauty of nature, the colossal expanse of the heavens, which make my paltry concerns of such little importance. Then my eye is drawn to the vapour trails from a dozen or more inter-continental passenger jets. We live slightly to the west of the flight path for planes coming in from North America and it's very busy early in the morning.

I can't hear the planes and I can only just see them, tiny silver specks against the blue, but the trails reach back miles and there are dozens of them, catching the morning sun and contrasting strongly with the blue sky. We've all seen them, but because Judy and I live on a hill and can see a great distance, I can see a lot of them all at once.

During these moments I don't go into medievalist mode and think, 'They are evil, a sign of the devil, the world has gone mad, we must stop now and all live in rattan huts and eat raw vegetables.' I think of the people on board excited at the prospect of the end of their long-haul flight. I have flown around the world so many times, stared out of the window at the landscape below and felt spiritually uplifted. The technology that allows us to move around like that is amazing; we all take it for granted, but I am still impressed.

More and more of us are becoming aware that the impact such forms of travel has on the world could be quite impressive, as in we are making a bit of a mess of it. So what do we do, stop flying? Hello, anyone there, are we really going to stop flying? I don't think so. We may have to when it gets so expensive, but in my experience (50-odd years etc.) it has got steadily cheaper and cheaper to fly, until now you can actually get on a plane for virtually nothing. How crazy is that?

I think we can hope that most people will fly a bit less often and think about it a little bit more. Of course we can change, because we're middle class and we care, but the emerging nations of India and China will want to fly about like we have, and there's a lot of them and quite a few have got a lot of money.

I have this abiding image of a genuinely caring Californian or Canadian man. He will be in his early forties and he does a lot of trekking in the woods, he wears sensible, unfashionable clothes and knows a great deal about nature. He will eat locally produced organic food and he possibly wears his hair in a ponytail, but he's not a lazy hippie, he's a really committed and busy environmental activist. His house is tidy and made of wood. His computer will be made by Apple. He really does care about the environment and he is very well informed. He's had a great education and he knows what is going on. He is a purist and a descendant of the original Protestant European settlers in North America. He thinks flying is wrong and he no longer does it. If he has a car it will be a hybrid and he will look at and internally criticize the vast majority of North Americans who still drive absurdly inefficient cars.

I have the feeling that even this man, with his privileged education and fortunate birthplace, i.e. the richest country on earth, with his benign view of nature and man's place in it, is probably starting to feel that his struggles are a bit hopeless.

I certainly felt that for most of my year of not buying anything. What on earth was the point? I wasn't making any difference to anything. I knew that my mere existence was causing more damage than any action I took could make amends for. Yet there was hope in what I did, that's what I came to realize. If there isn't hope, there's no point getting up in the morning. The human race lives on hope; it's one of the vital ingredients in life. The list should really read: food, shelter, clothing and hope. I have to hope that my small change has made a difference, even if it is only inside me.

After becoming better informed about the questions being asked by more and more people around the globe, I think this tiny spark of hope is spreading. I now believe there is a general consensus emerging that the way we consume is unsustainable and, more importantly, temporary. It just cannot go on at the level we are experiencing at the moment; the laws of physics dictate that something has to change. So I didn't end my year in despair. I felt battered and bowed, but not without hope.

Scrapped

DEC
19
2007

I CATCH the train to London about once a week when I am recording the voice-overs for *Scrapheap Challenge*. The journey goes in no time if I am writing and this chapter was written on the train.

I attended my last recording on 25 November. *Scrapheap Challenge* has been on telly a long time. During my year of making do, we recorded the tenth and, for me, final series of the show. *Scrapheap Challenge*, it's bonkers, bigger, bolder, better and badder than ever. We like to alliterate on *Scrapheap Challenge*, 'a stupendous stampede of steaming scrap is speeding your way!'

In the biz it's referred to as Lads and Dads telly, which I think is a very good illustration of the strange world broadcasters inhabit. They like to pigeonhole a show and that's our particular hole. You can't really argue with it, as I have met countless lads and dads who watch it, but I always

243

remember the charming Sikh man who came up to me in the street and said his kids never missed a show. I automatically assumed they would be lads. I was wrong. Four smartly dressed girls from about seven to 14 appeared around the corner and started gabbling excitedly about every episode they'd seen, which one was their favourite, and do we put things on the heap, and who were the best team, and do I love Lisa Rogers?

The show does seem to have made an impact in the throw-away world of popular culture. There's a whole generation of kids who have grown up with it. They know it's possible to bodge something together because they've seen the teams do it. In my quiet moments I've pondered on the possibility that one or two of these kids will grow up to become engineers and work on some truly revolutionary invention which will actually change the world for the better. Obviously it's possible one will grow up and work for the military, be very well paid, have a limitless budget and develop a better method for killing people. Something like the legendary 'lazy gun' imagined by Iain M. Banks in his sci-fi novel *Against a Dark Background*. You don't have to aim the lazy gun or anything tiresome like that; you fire it any old where and the bullets always find their target. Nice.

I don't know how influential *Scrapheap Challenge* has been on my life and outlook, but I've certainly spent a lot of time around the seriously colossal heaps of rubbish we throw away.

The first seven years we made *Scrapheap Challenge* we did film in real working scrapyards, from Brentford to Canning Town in London, then to Los Angeles and then to an idyllic heap just outside Reading. They varied in size but they had one thing in common: they were full of relatively contemporary trash.

For the last three years we made the series on an army base in Hampshire and imported hundreds of tons of top-quality hand-picked rubbish to create our own scrapheap. Strangely, it was impossible to tell it apart from a real one.

What was immediately obvious to me as I stumbled around the set is that the machines we make for ourselves don't last very long. I don't mean the creations the teams produce on the show, I mean the ones that had once been bought as gleaming examples of modernism in a showroom. I suppose previously I had imagined a scrapyard to be full of stuff from the Victorian era, old mangles and galvanized washtubs. It was the newness of the stuff that was piled up all around that was the most shocking.

When a car has been turned on its roof and piled up in a corner, it loses all its dignity, its charm, its flair and attractiveness. Doesn't matter what make or what badge it once proudly wore, it becomes a mucky encumbrance and an embarrassment to the human race. What we saw every day on that show was the underbelly of the industrial revolution, the casually discarded dream of modernity.

It is no longer the case that people are sad at the loss of a much-loved car. At one time, certainly when I was a child, a family had a more intimate and personal relationship with something like a car. The dad would tinker with it, the mum might put seat covers over the knackered fabric, the kids might give it a name and then, after 15 or 20 years, after the son or daughter had learned to drive in it and when it had finally coughed its last gasp, it was towed off to the heap. The family would wave sadly at it as they watched it dragged away, and in later years they might see the car featured in the background of a family snap and remember it fondly.

Or maybe that was just my family and my mum's old black Morris Minor. It's sentimental nonsense, I know, but the exposure I have had to the torrent of trash on the heap has made me extra sensitive to such events. I would sometimes look at the remnants of a car door, crushed under a massive steel beam and a load of old computers, and think, 'A little child once slept leaning against that door on a journey back from Granny's house.' A bit soppy, maybe, but we had very long days on *Scrapheap Challenge* and occasionally my mind used to wander.

The show was one of those flukes of broadcasting. We started making it in 1998, around the time I had been involved with two other quirky, one-off TV series that were fun to make but I was convinced no one would ever watch.

One was called *I Camcorder*, which was devised by the writers of *Red Dwarf* and encouraged people to use their video cameras a little more creatively. I know some people must have watched this, because I've since worked with a director whose mum allowed him to stay up to watch the series as a special privilege. When you hear that sort of story over lunch, it can make you feel a little well worn.

The other was called *Hollywood Science*, a show that used scenes from big Hollywood movies to explain various scientific phenomena. A good example was the Keanu Reeves movie *Speed*, in which Sandra Bullock makes a bus jump over the gap in the freeway flyover. Could she really do it? Answer: not really.

Scrapped

My co-host on *Hollywood Science*, the wonderful Jonathan Hare, got his complicated calculator out and did maths at a level I can't even describe. He worked out it would be possible to make a 6-ton bus jump a 25-yard gap in a flyover, if it was travelling at over 700,000 miles an hour. Fun stuff.

So to my mind, as we finished recording the first series of *Scrapheap Challenge* in 1998, I had made another of these quirky one-off shows which some people watch but not enough to sustain them. Ten years and something like 150 episodes later, I have to admit I was wrong. *Scrapheap Challenge* is shown in dozens of countries and has a huge following across all ages, genders, races and interestingly class barriers. I have met well-rough individuals with extreme facial hair and motorbikes in their kitchens who love it, and staggeringly posh people with actual titles who never miss a show.

It clearly taps into something in the psyche. I can't really narrow it down to the British psyche, because for all our preconceptions about American consumerism, we met some seriously brilliant bodgers, or kludgers as they call themselves, in America.

I think there is a very basic human drive to try and fix things when they are broken, from patching a pair of trousers or darning a pair of socks, something I did a fair bit of during my year of making do, to mending a puncture on a bike or changing the engine in an old car.

This is possibly why *Scrapheap Challenge* has worked so well; it is very firmly attached to the period.

When I first had a car, its internal gubbins were really only two steps away from a Meccano set, something I grew up with and spent hundreds of hours making things with. If I spent long enough looking at the engine of my Morris van, I could clearly see how it worked and what might be wrong with it. The technology was simple, sparse, fairly crude and very repairable. I'm not saying it was better; in fact in many ways those old cars were dangerous, as the brakes worked sporadically and the engines unreliably. They were also highly polluting and uneconomical.

The technology and design of internal combustion engines has developed and improved to a huge extent, but this has resulted in the ability to bodge, fix up and mend cars being taken away from the average Joe.

My hybrid car is a classic example. When I open the bonnet to top up the screen wash, there are two large silvery metal things joined together with a dense tangle of thick and intimidating-looking wire. I think one of these lumps is an internal combustion engine and the other is a 44-horsepower electric motor, although it's hard to be sure which is which. There are also numerous black boxes full of computer equipment stuffed under the bonnet which I wouldn't even know how to open, far less to tinker with. Under the driver and passenger seats there are further black boxes which have connector sockets on them the likes of which I have never seen elsewhere. I assume they are for plugging into laptops at the service centre so that every last nodule of the car's system can be checked in seconds.

The idea that I could in some way 'tinker' with this vehicle is a bad joke. I am a bit of a nerdy geek, I've researched it, looked at manufacturer's drawings of the bizarre transmission system and I truly haven't got a clue how it works. This is all fine until it breaks, and anything that humans make breaks, that's just what happens.

So when stuff like this breaks we don't have much choice – we can either throw it away or take it somewhere to be fixed. And that's just a car. What about a tumble dryer or a washing machine, a water heating system or a pressure washer. There are fewer and fewer products that many of us use on a regular basis that we have any understanding of or chance of fixing ourselves.

This is the niche where *Scrapheap Challenge* fits. The programme shows that things can be bodged together, that there is still the chance of making something yourself, even if it is only intended to work for three minutes. I think we know we can never do this in our everyday lives, so the contestants do it for us.

After ten years of watching other people bodging with brilliance, it has almost totally removed my confidence in doing stuff like that myself. I now have a fairly comprehensive knowledge of mechanical engineering. I could describe to you how an automatic transmission system works, or the internal pressure created by a turbo system on a diesel engine. I know why wings on aeroplanes work and what makes a digger's hydraulic arm able to move big piles of dirt. But I couldn't make them and I probably couldn't fix them if they broke.

That said, the upside is I now have an address book stuffed with numbers for people who can make or fix pretty much anything I need.

The Final Irony

DEC
23
2007

THE VERY last thing I expected to find when my year of not buying anything ended was that I now couldn't buy anything because of dire financial planning in the past.

What had kept me going through the latter part of the year was the acceptance that this was an experiment, born not out of necessity but from a desire to reconnect with what is really important in life. In most ways I was successful in this, but I admit that towards the end of the year I was thinking to myself, 'When the year is finally over I'm going straight out to the shops to get the new so-and-so.'

So, at the end of the year I bought four pairs of new socks, five pairs of new underpants, two new T-shirts and one pair of trousers in a sale. The reason for this rather meagre shopping spree was that we hit a painful situation just after Christmas.

The best and most honest description is we were up the creek financially.

The Final Irony

Everyone has to worry about money and income in one way or another, but people like me who are self-employed have to plan ahead with almost military precision. I don't receive a salary or a regular weekly wage. I can sometimes go for months without earning a penny. I once had a meeting with my bank manager, a very nice man called Nigel, to try and borrow more money to pay for the endless development of our house. The worrying thing was he was quite happy to lend me more than I asked for. This was a few years ago. I understand the situation with loans, mortgages and the like has changed a bit recently.

During our discussion he drew me a graph of what another client's bank balance would look like over a year. This was someone on a regular monthly salary and the graph resembled a child's drawing of the sea: big regular waves running neatly across the page. Money comes in at the start of the month and then slowly ebbs away until the start of the next month. How reassuring must that be; I have never experienced it. Then he showed me a printout of my own graph. It looked a little like a drawing of the sea done by someone who wears a shirt with very, very long sleeves and who dribbles a little too much to mix in regular society. He was impressed with the way I handled my finances, because there was no pattern to base decisions on. How right he was, no pattern whatsoever, just the reliable stability of chaos. I explained to Nigel that my ability to cope with this mayhem was down to long and bitter experience.

So, three years before I made my non-consuming commitment, we were consuming like newly rich Chinese corporate bosses. Not cars and consumer goods, but building materials. We spent 18 months 'doing up our house'. What a jolly old nightmare it was, living in a rented holiday home while the house we had lived in for 15 years was comprehensively gutted, the garden we had nurtured and cared for was turned into an open-cast mine and landfill site covered in diggers, white vans and rubble. Everything we owned was stored in a damp garage and covered in musty tarpaulins. But we did it and when it was finished friends and family were suitably impressed. Not the kids, of course – the first night we were back in our pristine and newly finished house my son claimed he preferred it the way it was before. Oh, the joy they bring.

Throughout this stressful and chaotic period I was very busy earning a living and pouring every last penny into the house project. I was trying desperately not to borrow yet more money and fought frantically to pull back on the reins of expenditure as the chippies nailed, the plasterers plastered and the plumber plumbed. What a fool! That didn't last long and we eventually had to up the mortgage a tad. I generally hate the word tad, but in this instance it's great. This particular tad was in fact a massive fiscal chunk, but tad sounds so much less painful. As I have already mentioned, I hate borrowing money, and when we sat in the garden during the first summer with the newly finished house I felt a warm glow of pride that we had done so much and not had to borrow a king's ransom.

Then the tax bill landed on the rather lovely and painfully expensive stone floor in the entrance hall. After 30 years as a self-employed person, 30 years carefully putting half my income aside for just such an event and suddenly, wham. A tax bill to write home about. A tax bill that wiped us out. A tax bill that immediately spun our once secure position on to a knife edge of budget balancing.

Now, before I go any further I want to make it clear that I am not moaning about paying tax. I think it is absolutely right that I should pay it. I benefit directly from the society I live in, from the infrastructure and support systems that have been built up for hundreds of years by working people paying tax. I am also not moaning about paying too much tax. You get a tax bill like I received simply because you have earned a lot of money, so obviously the only real solution for wealthy people who moan on and on about high taxes is to earn less money.

I also want to take this opportunity to remind ourselves of the obvious truth that really, really rich people don't pay tax. They employ enough people to wangle out of it. They are the famous 'non-doms', who lie their way out of paying tax by saying they live somewhere else and pay tax there. Like the Cayman Islands, where there are just about three houses, a posh hotel, 4,000 banks and a tax rate of 2 per cent.

It's mugs like me and you who pay tax, who are honest about it and don't try and wangle their way out of it, or indeed cannot afford to wangle their way out of it. The one time I had an inspection from Customs and Excise they gave me money! I had overpaid and they worked it out by going through every scrap of paper in my office for three days. When they had finished they had kindly piled up all the old love letters Judy had written to me from Australia that they had found in my invoice file. I knew those letters were somewhere.

So, I don't moan about tax, but that doesn't mean it doesn't hurt when you write out the cheque. They are, without question, the biggest cheques I ever write, and I am an idiot in some ways not to have used that money on capital expenditure. I could have bought my own TV studio and claimed it back. OK, a small regional TV studio. Or a really nice camera and claimed some of it back. But I didn't. I spent it on concrete and MDF and didn't claim anything and there's an end to it.

The other alternative is, as I said, to earn less money, not to work so hard, to spend more time with your children if you have them, or help in other ways in your community for no money. At the end of the year you will have done some good and your tax bill will be piddling.

This is my intention and so far I'm doing really well at it. In fact, without planning or thought, I am embarking on a year of earning less. This is not entirely self-imposed, because at the time of writing, for the first time for 20-odd years, I don't have a job, like a big proper job with a guaranteed income. I've got thousands of jobs, as in gigs, little events, voice-overs and short-term TV shows. So in effect I have had the decision made for me, which doesn't quite feel the same as making it yourself. I admit it's not as directly challenging to the consumer hegemony as consuming less, and it's very much more challenging for my high-maintenance family, but it might mean I get a bit more time to do what I really want to do.

Then you are faced with that particular internal challenge: what do I really want to do? Which is when I realize how lucky I am, because I already do pretty much what I want to do, and I get paid for it, and after I get paid I have to pay tax on what I earn.

I think I want a break from it all but I know I can't. I'm on that blasted wheel and I can't get off without smashing it, and smashing the wheel doesn't affect only me, it affects people I love, help support and care for. I have nothing to fall back on without selling everything we own and living in a tent. A second-hand tent, in the garden of someone who doesn't mind us living there.

Every last penny of our savings, all the SIPS, SATS, SOTS, TESSAS and TOSSAS, or whatever those tax-free savings things are called, have already been cashed in and used up. I managed to pay the tax bill and not go to debtors' jail, but it was close.

So that painful experience was in the background during my year of making do, and in the autumn I got the letter from my accountants informing me of the next expected tax burden for the January payment. As Christmas approached I knew we weren't going to be able to make it. I wasn't going to be able to go on an extravagant spending spree and prance about in a new hand-made suit I had to pay for.

My patient and slightly scary wife says she finds it disturbing when I talk about money or the chronic lack of it because I keep laughing. It's true, I find it funny. Is it the irony of the whole thing? I don't know, but it does tickle me. It's possible that by the time you read this the smile will have been firmly wiped off my face. A year without buying anything, when I had the money to buy quite a lot, followed by a year during which I would quite like to buy a couple of specific things and I can barely pay the gas bill. Somehow it all seems entirely appropriate.